Apologies from Death Row

I0123545

Apologies from Death Row explores the notion of remorse, apologies, and forgiveness within the context of capital punishment in the United States, through the final words of offenders on death row, and the covictims' responses to them in their statements to the press after witnessing the execution.

The book demonstrates that there is evidence that some offenders on death row are truly remorseful and that some of the family members of their victims could benefit from this remorse, but that this is unlikely in the current system of capital punishment. Drawing from the fields of criminology, psychology, and sociology, the book begins with a theoretically informed introduction to the concepts of remorse and forgiveness, followed by an exploration of apology and forgiveness specifically in the context of capital punishment. It discusses how some initiatives within the criminal justice system, such as apology laws and restorative justice programmes, are being used to make it easier for offenders to apologize to their victims. Offenders on death row are considered, addressing why they might or might not apologize, and whether they are even capable of showing true remorse. The book then considers the family members of their victims ("covictims"), addressing whether they benefit from hearing the offender express remorse and witnessing the execution, and whether forgiveness is possible in this context. Evidence to support the arguments presented in the book come from the offenders' final words and the covictims' responses to them in their statements to the press. The book dispels two common myths about the death penalty. First, it shows that offenders on death row are not simply "monsters" who are incapable of understanding the severity of their crimes. Second, it provides evidence that, despite the popular belief that the death penalty is necessary in order to provide closure for the victims' family members, it may actually have the opposite effect. The family members' statements to the press after witnessing the execution contain more negative themes like anger and disappointment than positive themes like closure and peace. The book concludes with a discussion of the implications this has for systems of justice in general, and how a better understanding of the emotional state of offenders can help both victims and offenders.

Apologies from Death Row will be of great interest to students and scholars of Criminology, Psychology, and Sociology.

Judy Eaton is a Professor of Psychology at Wilfrid Laurier University, Canada. She did her graduate work in social psychology at York University, receiving her MA in 2000 and PhD in 2005. Prior to that, she earned BAs in English and Psychology at McMaster University. The main focus of Professor Eaton's research is the causes, consequences, and resolution of interpersonal conflict. Using a social cognitive framework, her research examines the role of apology and other gestures of remorse in facilitating forgiveness. In the context of the criminal justice system, she has studied remorse in offenders on death row, the concept of closure as it relates to victims of crime, and how victims of crime are viewed (and influenced) by third parties (i.e., people not involved in the crime).

Routledge Studies in Criminal Behaviour

For more information about this series, please visit: https://www.routledge.com/
Routledge-Studies-in-Criminal-Behaviour/book-series/RSCB

Apologies from Death Row

The Meaning and Consequences
of Offender Remorse

Judy Eaton

Routledge
Taylor & Francis Group

LONDON AND NEW YORK

First published 2024
by Routledge
4 Park Square, Milton Park, Abingdon, Oxon OX14 4RN

and by Routledge
605 Third Avenue, New York, NY 10158

Routledge is an imprint of the Taylor & Francis Group, an informa business

© 2024 Judy Eaton

The right of Judy Eaton to be identified as author of this work has been asserted in accordance with sections 77 and 78 of the Copyright, Designs and Patents Act 1988.

All rights reserved. No part of this book may be reprinted or reproduced or utilised in any form or by any electronic, mechanical, or other means, now known or hereafter invented, including photocopying and recording, or in any information storage or retrieval system, without permission in writing from the publishers.

Trademark notice: Product or corporate names may be trademarks or registered trademarks, and are used only for identification and explanation without intent to infringe.

British Library Cataloguing-in-Publication Data
A catalogue record for this book is available from the British Library

ISBN: 978-1-032-47179-2 (hbk)
ISBN: 978-1-032-47181-5 (pbk)
ISBN: 978-1-003-38494-6 (ebk)

DOI: 10.4324/9781003384946

Typeset in Times New Roman
by Newgen Publishing UK

Contents

Tables

Preface

This book examines the concept of remorse in the unique context of death row. As a social psychologist who studies interpersonal conflict, my interest is in how the underlying principles of how humans resolve conflict are manifested in the extreme context of capital punishment. While I do not personally support capital punishment, a critique of the morality, effectiveness, or practicality of capital punishment is beyond the scope of this book.

This book incorporates quotes from the last statements of offenders and from statements made to the press by the loved ones of the victims. The offender's names are provided with their quotes – these are a matter of public record, and this allows interested readers to seek out more details about their cases. However, when quotes from the family members of victims are included, their names are not provided. This is in no way an effort to silence their voices or force them to remain anonymous in a system that already tends to ignore victims. Although their quotes also came from published sources, the decision was made to not include their names in an effort to respect and protect their privacy.

Acknowledgements

The analyses in this book are based on a very large amount of sometimes very hard-to-find data, and I am incredibly grateful to Melissa Handford and Kassandra Roul for helping to collect, organize, and code all of the statements. I would also like to thank Anna Theuer and Tony Christensen, who were my co-authors on two of the earlier projects on which this book is based. My collaborations with them have helped shape some of the ideas in this book. I'm also grateful to Dawood Ahmad, Scott Annandale, Kelsey Ioannani, and Thomas Leite, who helped with the data collection and coding for those earlier projects. This research was funded, in part, by a grant from the Social Sciences and Humanities Research Council of Canada. I also thank the staff at Routledge, who have been helpful and supportive at every stage of this book, and the anonymous reviewers, who improved the book with their insightful comments and suggestions. Finally, I thank Scott and Lauren, for their love and support at the starting line, the finish line, and all points in between.

1 Remorse and forgiveness in the criminal justice system

In 2017, immediately before he was executed in Arkansas for the murder of four individuals, Kenneth Williams gave a final statement in which he apologized to the families of his victims. His actions were wrong, senseless, and inexcusable, he said, and he acknowledged the pain he had caused them. He said he hoped that his execution would bring them peace and closure. He acknowledged that he could not go back and undo what he had done, but that he was a different person than he was back then. Then, in his last words before being injected with the drugs that would end his life, he asked for their forgiveness (Chavez, 2017).

On the day of the execution, Kayla Greenwood, the daughter of one of Williams' victims, wrote a letter to the governor of Arkansas asking for Williams' life to be spared. His death would not ease the family's pain, she explained, and it was not what they wanted. Instead of helping them heal, the family felt that his execution would make them feel worse. After their initial request to meet with Williams had been denied, they paid for his daughter to fly out to see him and attend his execution. Through her they learned of his redemption while in prison, and how it manifested in the help he offered others who were struggling with similar traumatic upbringings as his. Greenwood ended her letter with another request to meet with Williams, so that the family could tell him face-to-face that they forgave him. This, she said, would bring them closure (Greenwood, 2017). The request was denied, and Williams was executed that evening.

These statements were made in relation to a unique ritual in parts of the United States whereby individuals convicted of

DOI: 10.4324/9781003384946-1

capital murder and sentenced to death are permitted to make a last statement before being executed, and the family members of the murder victims are permitted to witness it. Their comments are interesting for a number of reasons: an offender who knows he has less than ten minutes left to live chooses to use his final words to apologize for his crime and ask for forgiveness; the family of one of the victims says that they have already forgiven him; and a formal request was made by the victims' family that he not be executed because it would make them feel worse.

This exchange challenges two common beliefs about capital punishment: First, that death row offenders are cold and remorseless monsters and second, that victims' family members need to witness the execution in order to gain a sense of closure and feel that justice has been served. Williams' last statement does not seem like the statement of a remorseless monster. He most likely knew that apologizing was not going to earn him a reprieve – it was too late. Why, then, did he make himself vulnerable by taking responsibility for his crime and asking for forgiveness? While we can never know his true intentions, his final words, offered when he had nothing left to lose, reveal his humanity. The family's request to spare Williams' life also does not seem like the statement of a family that is seeking closure through vengeance. Instead, they want an opportunity to tell him in person that they forgive him.

Many offenders on death row do not apologize for their crimes, and many of their victims' family members would not forgive them even if they did apologize. However, as the research and data presented in this book will show, exchanges like the one above happen often enough to suggest that offenders are not uniform in their lack of remorse and the family members of their victims do not necessarily benefit from seeing the offender be executed. This is important for the practice of capital punishment because it calls into question some of its key assumptions – that offenders are unrepentant and that only their death will bring the loved ones of their victims closure.

It is also important for justice systems in general. Although the United States is unique among developed Western democracies in its embrace of capital punishment, the issues raised – the dehumanizing of offenders, the notions of offender remorse and victim forgiveness, the role of emotions in the criminal justice system, and the potential for alternative forms of justice – are universal and not specific to the death penalty. By examining how these issues manifest in the extreme case of capital punishment we can better understand the needs and emotional states of offenders and victims in general.

Before exploring the expressions of remorse by offenders on death row and how these sentiments are viewed by the people who hear them, we first need to understand what remorse is. This chapter provides an introduction to the concepts of remorse and forgiveness, defining what they are and how they are used in the criminal justice system.

Remorse

Defining remorse

Consider the terms "remorse" and "apology." While they both may imply that an individual is sorry, these terms are not interchangeable. To be remorseful is to recognize the harm you have caused, to feel regret for both the act and the consequences, and to have a desire to make amends (Bandes, 2022). Remorse is an internal emotion that we feel after having caused harm. It can be expressed both verbally and non-verbally, or not at all. For example, an individual could express their remorse by stating that they are sorry and that they promise to make it up to the injured party, but they could also reveal their emotional state through their body language (e.g., by crying or bowing their head) or through their actions (e.g., trying to correct their mistake or deciding not to appeal a guilty verdict). They may feel remorseful but not say anything at all.

An apology is a verbal or written statement expressing regret or remorse for one's actions. While it might be an effective way to share feelings of remorse, the difference between remorse and apology is that remorse is an emotion, whereas an apology is simply one way that remorse can be communicated. The two are not mutually inclusive: An individual who says, "I'm sorry" is not necessarily experiencing remorse, in the same way that an individual who does not apologize is not necessarily unremorseful. As we'll see, this makes the study of remorse in the criminal justice system complicated because it can be very difficult to assess an individual's true emotional state. When there are benefits to appearing remorseful (such as a lighter prison sentence), an offender might be tempted to fake remorse, and even judges with years of experience sometimes are unable to accurately determine if an offender is truly remorseful (Bandes, 2022).

The role of apologies in remorse

An apology is one of the most common methods for us to let the person we hurt know that we feel sorrow or regret over our actions. A simple "I'm sorry," however, is not usually enough. While there are many ways to apologize, researchers generally agree that the basic elements of a good apology include an expression of sorrow (i.e., "I'm sorry"), taking responsibility for the harm done, an attempt to make amends, and a promise that it will not happen again (Scher & Darley, 1997). These elements do not contribute equally to the value of the apology. Often, the most important aspect of the apology is taking responsibility for the offence. Simply saying the words "I'm sorry" do not effectively demonstrate that you understand what you did and why it caused harm, and it might leave the person you hurt saying, "for what?".

Consider these two apologies, each offered by an individual on death row, offered to the family members of their victims:

> I'm sorry for everyone I've hurt.
> (Andrew DeYoung, executed Georgia in 2011)

> I cannot wait to finish paying this debt I owe so I can apologize to the souls of Mr. Morgan and Mr. Bullard, and ask them to forgive me for my taking their lives... To the families of my victims all I can say is I'm sorry for the pain I've caused you. I hope my death will bring you some peace.
> (Michael Delozier, executed in Oklahoma in 2009)

Even though the first apology does include the words "I'm sorry," DeYoung does not explain what he is sorry for, or even who the target of his apology is. While he may have been remorseful, this apology does not effectively communicate that he understood what he did and who it affected. The second example is a much more complete apology. Delozier is specific about the harm he caused and the pain it has caused the victims' families. He sees his execution as a way to repay his debt by giving him the opportunity to ask for forgiveness directly from his victims (in the afterlife).

Some apologies, rather than taking responsibility for the harm done, include denials of responsibility. For example, the person who committed the harm might make an excuse ("I'm sorry but I was drunk and didn't realize what I was doing"), blame the victim ("I'm sorry but he shouldn't have fought back"), downplay the seriousness of the act ("I'm sorry but it wasn't that bad"), or even apologize for the victim's response to the offence ("I'm sorry you're mad"). Although each of these examples includes the words "I'm sorry," those words do not carry much meaning to victims, especially when followed by the word "but." Rather than make the recipient of the apology feel better, apologies like these can actually make them more angry and less likely to accept the apology. A good apology is outwardly focused: It demonstrates concern for the victim and regret and sorrow for the harm that has been caused to them, and not simply regret for having got caught for committing the harmful act. As Weisman (2009) states, "for his or her claim to be validated, the wrongdoer must suffer for the suffering that he caused rather than for the suffering he has endured" (p. 58).

The non-verbal aspects of remorse

A good apology can be a clear signal of remorse, but in addition to the words themselves, the way they are said matters too. Imagine an apology that contains all the "right" words, but the person offering it is smiling, looks bored, or is speaking without any emotion at all. A verbal apology alone will not necessarily be convincing – the harm-doer must also show that they are remorseful. Non-verbal displays of remorse, termed "embodied remorse" (Hornsey et al., 2020), could be actions such as crying, bowing one's head, or kneeling, or they could more subtle gestures like a small change in facial expression. Research shows that offenders who "embody" their remorse by crying, looking sad, and generally appearing to be feeling sorrow are perceived as being more remorseful and sincere (Picó et al., 2020; ten Brinke & Adams, 2015), are more likely to elicit empathy in observers (Halmesvaara et al., 2020), and are believed to be less likely to reoffend (Hornsey et al., 2020).

There are a few reasons why embodied remorse is so effective at demonstrating the actual feelings of the offender. First, it shows that the offender is experiencing shame (Halmesvaara et al., 2020) and that they feel guilt and sorrow for the harm they have caused. Shame and guilt are considered to be "moral emotions" (Haidt, 2003) and they are often seen as being key to promoting prosocial and altruistic behaviour while inhibiting antisocial behaviour (Tangney et al., 2011). Showing remorse demonstrates that the offender recognizes that what they did was wrong, and that they join the community in condemning the wrongful act (Weisman, 2009).

A second reason why embodied remorse is effective is that it "mak[es] the suffering visible" (Weisman, 2004, p. 125). An apology on its own may not be able to convey this same message because it provides less information about how the person offering the apology is actually feeling. They might be reciting an apology that someone else has written for them, or they might be particularly good at "reading the room" and anticipating what the harmed party wants to hear. Because physical displays of remorse are less easy (although not impossible) to fake than simply saying the words that cover all the components of an effective apology, they can provide clues as to the sincerity of their apology (Hornsey et al., 2020). Even small physical cues and subtle facial expressions can help observers make intuitive judgments about whether some is remorseful. For instance, Funk and colleagues (2017) found that raters were most likely to determine that someone looked remorseful when the inner corners of their eyebrows were raised or their lips went down slightly at the ends. Thus, while not infallible, body language can act as a type of lie detector when it comes to remorse.

A third reason why physical displays reinforce perceptions of remorse is that they indicate vulnerability on the part of the offender. When a remorseful offender appears to be physically suffering we tend to view their apology as being more "costly" to them. Verbally admitting our mistakes and taking full responsibility for them is a way of *saying* that are aware that we violated the basic social contract to act morally. However, the embodiment of remorse, such as bowing one's head, kneeling, and crying, *shows* that we are aware of our moral transgression and is seen as a sign of submission (Strayer & Trudel, 1984) – an act of physically lowering oneself to be beneath the wronged party. Research suggests that more effortful apologies are perceived as being more genuine than less effortful ones (Ohtsubo et al., 2012), and hence apologies that are supported by appropriate physical gestures might be viewed as more sincere or authentic.

There are even instances when an embodiment of remorse on its own might be the most effective and powerful indicator or remorse, without the need for a verbal apology. Hornsey and colleagues (2020) use the example of Willy Brandt, who was the Chancellor of the German Federal Republic. In 1970, Brandt was visiting a memorial in Warsaw to honour the Jewish victims of the Ghetto Uprising. Brandt was scheduled to lay a wreath on the site but unexpectedly, after adjusting a ribbon on the wreath, he dropped to his knees, bowed his head, and remained there, silently. His gesture is considered by some to have been more effective at conveying Germany's remorse for the atrocities in Poland than the well-crafted apologies made by other politicians (Hille et al., 2020).

Apologies and remorse in the criminal justice system

Apologizing is not easy. Depending on the severity of the harm done, there could be significant psychological costs to apologizing properly. The person who committed the harm must admit that they did something wrong or bad, which can make them feel embarrassed and ashamed (Exline & Baumeister, 2000; Tangney et al., 1992). In addition, there's no guarantee that the apology will be accepted – it could result in a negative response from the victim, which could make the harm-doer feel even worse (Dhami, 2016). As difficult as apologizing can be for non-criminal offences, the potential costs for criminal offenders are even higher. To apologize properly by taking responsibility for their actions, the offender must essentially admit that they are guilty. Even though there are laws in place that can make it less risky, from a legal perspective, for offenders to apologize, there are still reasons why they might be reluctant to do so. While the courts may not legally be able to hold the offender accountable if they apologize, this does not mean that the victim and/or the general public won't. Especially in public trials for more serious crimes, an offender might be reluctant to take responsibility for the crime because they are concerned about their public image. The fear of reproach has been shown to reduce the likelihood of an offender apologizing (Hodgins & Liebeskind, 2003; Struthers et al., 2008), so if they are afraid of being judged negatively by the victim and the community/general public, deciding to apologize might be especially difficult.

In addition, even if they do want to apologize, it might be a challenge for offenders to do so. Unless offenders seek contact with victims on their own (in cases where they are not prohibited from doing so), often the only time an offender has the opportunity to address the victim is in the courtroom right before being sentenced. The timing of this is far from ideal. Most importantly, the victim may not be present. An apology offered to a judge is not the same as an apology offered directly to the person harmed (Shapland et al., 2006). Even if the victim is present, if the offender wants to apologize they must do so in front of the entire courtroom. This can be especially humiliating if the apology is rejected (Bibas & Bierschbach, 2004; Tavuchis, 1991). In addition, victims may be sceptical about an apology that is offered immediately before the judge determines the sentence (Dillon, 2022; Petrucci, 2002). Thus, even if the offender is truly remorseful, it might be difficult for them to convince anyone of this.

For those offenders who are truly remorseful, there are definite benefits. Remorse can alleviate their feelings of guilt (Baumeister et al., 1994; Exline & Baumeister, 2000) and possibly even earn them forgiveness from their victims (Sherman et al., 2005); they can save face and project a more favourable impression of themselves (Darby & Schlenker, 1982; Goffman, 1971); and if they are religious it can help them make peace with their god (Simons, 2004).

Finding reliable data on how many offenders choose to apologize anyway, despite these challenges, is difficult. Apologies are common at sentencing hearings (Gruber, 2014), but the offender is expected to apologize at this stage, so their remorse may or may not be authentic. A cynical view of offender remorse might be that they only do it to reduce their sentences, and this may be true for some. The timing of the apology could make a difference, and if the offender offers it before the sentencing hearing, or after the sentencing is complete, it might be viewed as more sincere. For example, in 2012, a Canadian burglar in Guelph, Ontario left an anonymous note, along with the items he had stolen and $50 to pay for the screen door he had damaged, in which he stated, "I made the worst mistake of my life. I regretted it immediately afterwards…I can't put into words how sorry I am" (Edmiston, 2012).

Pro-remorse policies in the criminal justice system

The justice system seems to recognize the power of remorse (e.g., Braithwaite, 1989; Petrucci, 2002; Proeve & Tudor, 2016; Tudor et al., 2022), and yet it does not make it easy for offenders to apologize to their victims. However, there have been some positive changes in the justice system in recent years that provide better opportunities for offenders to demonstrate their remorse and for victims to actually benefit from that remorse. A detailed and exhaustive list is beyond the scope of this book, so we'll focus on the two most common practices: restorative justice and apology laws.

Restorative justice

Restorative justice is based on the assumption that crime involves offenders, victims, and the community, and thus all three should be involved in the justice process. Rather than acting as a means to administer punishment for laws that have been broken, restorative justice focuses on addressing the harm that has been done and finding ways to restore victims while also being sensitive to the needs of the offender (Zehr & Mika, 2017). It has its roots in Indigenous justice, which seeks to "restore balance within the community," which can only be accomplished by involving the entire community in the process (Hand et al., 2012, p. 452). Although apologies and subsequent forgiveness are not the primary goals of restorative justice, there are specific restorative justice practices that provide the opportunity for offenders to apologize directly to their victims. For example, in victim–offender mediation (sometimes called victim–offender conferences) the offender and victim meet, along with a trained facilitator, so that each can share their feelings about the crime, its aftermath, and what might have precipitated it (Hansen & Umbreit, 2018). Family group conferencing is similar, except it also involves family members and close others (Zehr, 2015). Circles extend beyond the family to the community and can include members of the traditional justice system such as the judge, police officers, and lawyers (Umbreit & Armour, 2010). Because the focus is on understanding rather than judgment or punishment, the offender has the opportunity express their remorse directly to the victim, and the victim has the opportunity to learn about the offender's history and circumstances, which might help them understand why they committed the crime.

Restorative justice programs make apologies easier because the offender has more opportunity to directly participate in the process and to interact with the victim. Some restorative justice programs have found high rates of apology from the offenders who participate in them, although the actual percentage of offenders who apologize in these programs varies a lot. For example, Dhami (2012), in a review of restorative justice programs in the United Kingdom, found that 36% of offenders apologized, while Sherman and colleagues (2005), in a comparative study of programs in the United Kingdom and Australia, reported apology rates of up to 100%. In these programs, whether the offender apologized depended on many factors, including the type of crime committed and the location, but overall, offenders were more likely to apologize when they participated in a restorative justice program than in the traditional justice system (Sherman et al., 2005). In fact, for some offenders, the desire to apologize was one of their main reasons for agreeing to participate in restorative justice (Hansen & Umbreit, 2018; Umbreit, 1994).

Apology laws

For an offender to apologize properly, they must take responsibility for the crime they committed. This presents a challenge for offenders who may not want to actually offer a guilty plea. Apology laws were developed to give offenders a chance to offer an apology without it being held against them by the legal system. While these laws are not universal, and they differ between countries and even within countries, their basic premise is that an apology made by or on behalf of an offender is not admissible in any trial or court proceeding – in other words, it allows them to apologize to the victim without consequence. Research has shown that victims who receive an apology are more likely to accept a settlement offer than those who do not (Robbennolt, 2006), so not only can these laws benefit victims who want an apology, but they can also result in less involvement by the criminal justice system and sometimes can prevent a lawsuit from being initiated by the victim against the offender (Heimreich, 2011).

For incarcerated offenders who want to apologize after the legal proceedings are complete, some jurisdictions in the United States offer "apology banks," where offenders can write and submit an apology letter to their victims. In many instances offenders are prohibited from contacting their victims; these banks provide an opportunity for them to apologize, but only if the victim provides consent. If the victim registers for the program, which indicates their willingness to receive an apology letter, they will be notified if their offender submits a letter, and it will be forwarded to them. While these types of program could be viewed as an insufficient substitute for proper victim–offender mediation (Restorative Justice International, 2014) and there is little data on their usage or effectiveness, they do provide an opportunity for offenders to reach out to their victims to express their remorse.

It is clear that some offenders are remorseful and would like to apologize, but this does not mean that they all are. It would be naïve to think that all offenders feel genuine remorse, or that if they do they are able to adequately convey this to victims. This means that any programs aimed to help facilitate offender apologies must recognize the diverse emotional response offenders might have after committing a crime including, for some, a complete lack of remorse.

Forgiveness

Defining forgiveness

If you were asked to explain what forgiveness means to you, you might mention terms such as letting go, forgetting, closure, mercy, peace, or reconciliation. Or you might mention that forgiveness is the *absence* of certain things, like anger, the desire for revenge, or a social debt. The challenge is, even though we generally have no trouble explaining our views on forgiveness, it seems there is little consensus on what it actually is (Kearns & Fincham, 2004). For instance, some people equate forgiving with forgetting, whereby in order to forgive something one must act like the event did not happen. Other people argue that to forget is to put yourself at risk of future harm, and that it is possible (and, indeed, preferable) to forgive while at the same time acknowledging that harm was done. Researchers have attempted to resolve this by formalizing a definition of forgiveness although, perhaps not surprisingly, even they do not agree completely on what it is. It is generally agreed that forgiveness is essentially an intrapersonal process. In other words, it is a change that happens within the victim, and does not require the involvement of the offender in order for it to occur (Brady et al., 2022). This means that it is possible to forgive someone who has not apologized or taken responsibility for the offence, which allows for forgiveness to occur even if an offender is deceased or otherwise unable to apologize.

The following definition encompasses the key elements of forgiveness as identified by researchers: Forgiveness is a deliberate and conscious decision to let go of one's legitimate anger towards a transgressor and to view him or her in a more positive way (Struthers et al., 2008). There are some key features of this definition worth noting. First, the definition states that forgiveness is a "deliberate and conscious decision." In other words, the harmed individual must make the decision to forgive on their own, and they should decide to forgive because they want to and not because they feel they should or because they are instructed to do so. Second, the definition states that forgiving involves giving up a *legitimate right* to be angry – forgetting the event happened, reframing it as not a transgression, or making excuses for the offender would simply transform the offence into something that does not require forgiveness. In order for forgiveness to be meaningful, there has to be a perceived need for it (Struthers et al., 2010), and forgetting, condoning, and excusing, rather than signifying forgiveness, only serve to reduce the *need* for forgiveness (Tavuchis, 1991). Third, the definition notes that forgiveness involves viewing the offender in a more positive way. This does not mean that the relationship is restored (if there was a prior relationship between the victim and the offender), but it does mean that the victim has softened their anger towards the offender. It involves a prosocial change towards the offender (Brady et al., 2022), but that does not necessarily mean replacing a negative opinion of the offender with a completely positive one.

The benefits of forgiveness

Forgiveness is sometimes considered to be a type of "gift" that victims bestow on the person who hurt them, but it is perhaps more accurately described as a gift that victims give themselves. While it is true that forgiveness can heal relationships and can bring a sense of peace to a truly remorseful offender, it can be said that the real benefactors of forgiveness are the victims. When he was released from prison after 27 years, anti-apartheid activist Nelson Mandela reportedly said, "As I walked out the door towards the gate that would lead to my freedom, I knew if I didn't leave my bitterness and hatred behind, I'd still be in prison" (Clinton, 2003, p. 236). The "bitterness and hatred" that Mandela mentions are common feelings after an offence, regardless of the intensity of the injustice. Being victimized hurts, and even if the offence did not involve any type of physical assault, the effects can be felt both emotionally and physically.

Feelings of anger and betrayal are common after being hurt by someone. Sometimes expressing this anger can be beneficial for victims because it can signal to the harm-doer that they committed an offence that caused pain, making them more motivated to try to make amends (Friedman et al., 2004). Thus, short-term anger can be adaptive because it can prompt conciliatory or remorseful behaviour (like an apology) from the offender. Long-term anger, however, can be harmful, both emotionally and physically. While we may think of anger as simply a negative emotion, it is actually a physiological response to threat. When we perceive something to be threatening (and that threat could be physical or emotional, real or imagined), our autonomic responses system is activated and gives us the tools to resist the threat. These tools include increased levels of stress hormones such as adrenaline and cortisol, which increase our heart rate and prepare our muscles for either "fight" (addressing the threat directly) or "flight" (escaping from the threat) (Cannon, 1932). In the short term these responses can be helpful – they could actually save our lives – but in the long term they can cause serious physical damage such as heart disease and stroke, chronic inflammation, and gastrointestinal disorders (VanItallie, 2002).

When we ruminate or obsess over a betrayal or offence it can feed into our anger, causing a prolonged and potentially harmful physical response (Alia-Klein et al., 2020). One way to stop this is to forgive. When we forgive and let go of our anger it not only frees up energy for more positive emotions (Ysseldyk et al., 2007) and improves our emotional well-being (Karremans et al., 2003) but there is evidence that it can also lead to improved physical health. Witvleit and colleagues (2001) found that thinking about revenge after a hurtful incident increased physiological stress responses such as heart rate and skin conductance, whereas thinking about forgiveness lowered these responses. These findings suggest that forgiveness, rather than vengeance, can result in better physical health. Other research has shown that people who are more forgiving in general tend to have better health, and this is partially due to the fact that they experience less anger and tend to deal with stress more effectively than those who tend to be less forgiving (Lawler et al., 2005). Forgiveness is considered to be an emotion-focused coping strategy, in that it can stop the spiral of negative emotions that can occur after a transgression, replacing the anger and stress with more positive emotions (Worthington & Scherer, 2004).

It's important to keep in mind that much of the research on forgiveness has been based on relatively minor interpersonal offences, conducted in very controlled settings, often using North American undergraduate students as participants (Tittler & Wade, 2019). While these studies can accurately identify the underlying mechanisms of forgiveness and the positive effects it can have on victims, their findings are not necessarily generalizable to all individuals in all situations. This book discusses remorse and forgiveness in the context of arguably the most severe offence one could commit – murder – and while there are many stories of victims who have forgiven even the most heinous crimes, there is less research on forgiveness in this area. This does not mean that the research discussed above is irrelevant to the serious offences that result in an individual being sentenced to death, but there is less evidence as to whether it does or not. Therefore, we need to acknowledge that, while there is no reason to suggest that the same theories of remorse and forgiveness that apply to less serious offences would not apply to more serious offences, we cannot just assume that it does.

Choosing not to forgive

Although there can be benefits to victims when they forgive, ultimately forgiveness is a personal decision. Remember that the definition of forgiveness states that forgiveness is a "deliberate and conscious" decision that must come from the victim. If they are not ready or willing to forgive, telling them to do so will not result in authentic forgiveness. In fact, it might do more harm than good, as making a victim feel like their response to an offence is not appropriate can be a form of revictimization (Eaton et al., 2022).

There are also some valid arguments for not forgiving under some conditions. In a series of studies that examined the daily interactions of heterosexual married couples, McNulty (2010; 2011) found that the partners who were forgiven were more likely to reoffend and be more psychologically and physically aggressive than the partners who were not forgiven. In addition, when one partner forgave the other for an offence, the other partner was more likely to engage in another offence the next day. In a subsequent research, McNulty has found that this tends to happen more with offending partners who score low on the personality trait of agreeableness (McNulty & Russell, 2016). Agreeableness, in the context of personality theory, is used to describe a set of prosocial tendencies and behaviours. Agreeable people tend to be kind, helpful, and considerate of others (Graziano & Eisenberg, 1997); people scoring low on this trait tend to be more self-focused and difficult to get along with. This suggests that most of the time forgiveness is not risky or foolish, but when we forgive people who are not motivated to reconcile or make amends it might be counterproductive, since it puts us at risk of being hurt again. Forgiving disagreeable people not only makes them more likely to reoffend, it can also affect how we feel about ourselves. When victims forgive partners who tend to be disagreeable and unwilling to make amends, the victims can experience a drop in self-respect and self-concept clarity, a phenomenon referred to as the "doormat effect" (Luchies et al., 2010).

Even if forgiveness is an ultimate goal, it takes time and effort. Forgiveness given without thought and careful consideration is not true forgiveness – Murphy (2007) refers to it as "cheap grace" (p. 33). It's also important to keep in mind that there is nothing inherently bad about feeling negative emotions. To advocate quick forgiveness in order to alleviate negative emotions like anger and resentment ignores the fact that some people might find comfort in embracing their anger and vindictive feelings (Lamb, 2002; Murphy, 2000). While there are documented benefits of forgiveness, it may not be the best decision in every situation.

Forgiveness in the criminal justice system: Restorative justice

Evidence from the research on restorative justice suggests that at least some victims are prepared to try to forgive their offenders. Victims do not have to participate in restorative justice programs, but many of them do, and studies show that they often do it specifically because they want an apology (Petrucci, 2002; Strang & Sherman, 2003). Some restorative justice programs report rates of forgiveness in victims as high as 75% (Sherman et al., 2005). These findings should be interpreted with caution, for two reasons. First, those victims who agree to participate in restorative justice programs may be more prepared to forgive than those who choose not to participate. It is possible that if they participate because they want an apology they may also be more open to the possibility of forgiveness. Second, restorative justice is used most often (although not exclusively) in criminal cases that are considered less severe, like property crime. One could argue that it's much easier to forgive someone who broke into your home and stole your television than someone who physically threatened you, so the high rates of forgiveness reported in the restorative justice literature might be, at least in part, due to the crimes being less serious and thus more forgivable. That isn't to say that more heinous crimes can't be forgiven – there are certainly stories of people who have forgiven offenders for the worst crimes imaginable (e.g., King, 2003), some of which will be discussed later in this book.

Learning about forgiveness in victims of crime who have not participated in a restorative justice program is more challenging because they often are not the focus of research studies. This might be partly due to the fact that they tend not to seek help after being victimized (McCart et al., 2010) and thus would be less likely to participate in a research study. However, there is evidence that, even without the benefits of a structured victim–offender mediation program, victims can come to forgive offenders (Field et al., 2013). A common theme among victims of crime who forgive their offenders is that they chose to forgive in order to benefit themselves, and not the offender (Cooney et al., 2011). Even if a victim might not be willing to forgive an offender, they may still benefit from receiving an apology. A victim might not be prepared to completely forgive an offender, but if the offender apologizes the victim might at least begin to see them as more human and stop being angry towards them (Umbreit et al., 1999). As we've seen, reducing anger has many benefits for victims.

Apologies, remorse, and forgiveness

There is a strong link between apology and forgiveness. In their meta-analysis of factors that can affect forgiveness, Fehr and colleagues (2010) synthesized the findings of 175 studies on forgiveness and found that, overall, an apology was one of the strongest predictors of forgiveness. A meta-analysis involves collecting all of the literature on a given topic and statistically combining the results in order to calculate the overall effect size, or importance, of the findings. Although not all apologies are equally effective (for example, "I'm sorry you're mad" will not likely lead to forgiveness), in general the link between apology and forgiveness is pretty robust.

One reason why we are more likely to forgive someone when they apologize is that when an offender appears to be remorseful we are more likely to feel empathy towards them (McCullough et al., 1997; 1998; Witvliet et al., 2020). Our first reaction to an offence might be anger and a desire to retaliate, but when the offender offers an apology it disrupts this natural desire for revenge. Remember that a good apology shows that the offender is suffering, and when they take responsibility and show true remorse it means they acknowledge that they violated a moral code. This humanizes the offender – it helps us view them not as an offender but as a person who made a mistake. When we can separate the act from the actor and see the offender as a decent person (Tavuchis, 1991) it makes it easier for us to feel empathy for them, which makes us less likely to retaliate and more likely to forgive.

Another reason why remorse leads to forgiveness is that it clarifies any uncertainty the victim might have about what caused the offence and who was at fault (Eaton et al., 2006). When someone hurts or betrays us, in addition to the emotional harm it causes, it can also make us confused. We might wonder why it happened and whether we did something to deserve it. Humans generally do not like uncertainty – it makes us feel threatened, defensive, and less motivated to forgive (Aquino & Douglas, 2003; Maltby & Day, 2004). When the offender apologizes and takes responsibility for the harm done, it helps eliminate this uncertainty, clarifying that the offender was at fault and confirms for us that we did not somehow deserve to be treated poorly. In fact, what validates us the most is the offender taking responsibility for what they did because that's the part of the apology that eliminates the uncertainty. Saying "I'm sorry" is actually less important than taking responsibility for the offence (Eaton et al., 2006).

In the context of the criminal justice system it would be unrealistic to assume that all offenders feel remorse or that offenders who do feel remorse will be forgiven. Even in non-criminal transgressions that is not always the case. However, we do know that remorse *can* make a difference in criminal cases. Victims are more likely to forgive an offender who they believe is remorseful (Umbreit & Vos, 2000; Witvliet et al., 2020), juries are more favourable in their decisions for offenders who appear to be remorseful (Bandes, 2016; Haney et al., 1994), and remorse is taken into account when making sentencing decisions, and often results in a lighter sentence (Berryessa, 2022; Rossmanith et al., 2018). Victims of crime who forgive report feeling better about themselves (Field et al., 2013) and tend to experience a stronger a sense of empowerment (Cooney et al., 2011). There are challenges, of course, with developing programs to facilitate offender apologies and victim forgiveness that are cost-effective, voluntary, and equitable, but the evidence presented in this chapter suggests that there is value in making the effort.

References

Alia-Klein, N., Gan, G., Gilam, G., Bezek, J., Bruno, A., Denson, T. F., … & Verona, E. (2020). The feeling of anger: From brain networks to linguistic expressions. *Neuroscience & Biobehavioral Reviews*, *108*, 480–497. https://doi.org/10.1016/j.neubiorev.2019.12.002

Aquino, K., & Douglas, S. (2003). Identity threat and antisocial behavior in organizations: The moderating effects of individual differences, aggressive modeling, and hierarchical status. *Organizational Behavior and Human Decision Processes*, *90*(1), 195–208. https://doi.org/10.1016/S0749-5978(02)00517-4

Bandes, S. A. (2016). Remorse and criminal justice. *Emotion Review*, *8*(1), 14–19. https://doi.org/10.1177/1754073915601222

Bandes, S. A. (2022). Remorse and judging. In S. Tudor, R. Weisman, M. Proeve, & K. Rossmanith (Eds.), *Remorse and criminal*

justice: Multi-disciplinary perspectives (pp. 19–39). Routledge. https//
doi.org/10.4324/9780429001062-3

Baumeister, R. F., Stillwell, A. M., & Heatherton, T. F. (1994). Guilt: An
interpersonal approach. *Psychological Bulletin*, *115*(2), 243–267. https://
doi.org/10.1037/0033-2909.115.2.243

Berryessa, C. M. (2022). Modeling "remorse bias" in probation
narratives: Examining social cognition and judgments of implicit
violence during sentencing. *Journal of Social Issues*, *78*(2), 452–482.
https://doi.org/10.1111/josi.12508

Bibas, S., & Bierschbach, R. A. (2004). Integrating remorse and apology
into criminal procedure. *The Yale Law Journal*, *114*, 85–148. https://doi.
org/10.2307/4135717

Brady, D. L., Saldanha, M. F., & Barclay, L. J. (2022). Conceptualizing
forgiveness: A review and path forward. *Journal of Organizational
Behavior*, *44*(2). https://doi.org/10.1002/job.2632

Braithwaite, J. (1989). *Crime, shame and reintegration.* Cambridge
University Press.

Cannon, W. B. (1932). *The wisdom of the body.* Norton.

Chavez, N. (2017, April 29). Kenneth Williams' execution. The last hours
leading to his death. *CNN.com*. https://edition.cnn.com/2017/04/29/us/
arkansas-kenneth-williams-timeline/index.html

Clinton, H. R. (2003). *Living history.* Simon and Schuster.

Cooney, A., Allan, A., Allan, M. M., Mckillop, D., & Drake, D. G. (2011).
The forgiveness process in primary and secondary victims of violent
and sexual offences. *Australian Journal of Psychology*, *63*(2), 107–118.
https://doi.org/10.1111/j.1742-9536.2011.00012.x

Darby, B. W., & Schlenker, B. R. (1982). Children's reactions to apologies.
Journal of Personality and Social Psychology, *43*(4), 742–753. https://
doi.org/10.1037/0022-3514.43.4.742

Dhami, M. K. (2012). Offer and acceptance of apology in victim-offender
mediation. *Critical Criminology*, *20*(1), 45–60. https://doi.org/10.1007/
s10612-011-9149-5

Dhami, M. K. (2016). Effects of a victim's response to an offender's
apology: When the victim becomes the bad guy. *European Journal of
Social Psychology*, *46*(1), 110–123. http://dx.doi.org/10.1002/ejsp.2145

Dillon, H. (2022). Cranking the sausage machine: A magistrate's perspective on remorse assessment. In S. Tudor, R. Weisman, M. Proeve, &
K. Rossmanith (Eds.), *Remorse and criminal justice: Multi-disciplinary
perspectives* (pp. 114–134). Routledge. https://doi.org/10.4324/978042
9001062-7

Eaton, J., Olenewa, J., & Norton, C. (2022). Judging "extreme"
forgivers: How victims are perceived when they forgive the unforgivable.

International Review of Victimology, *28*(1), 33–51. https://doi.org/
10.1177/02697580211028021

Eaton, J., Struthers, C. W., & Santelli, A. G. (2006). The mediating role of
perceptual validation in the repentance–forgiveness process. *Personality
and Social Psychology Bulletin*, *32*, 1389–1401. https://doi.org/10.1177/
0146167206291005

Edmiston, J. (August 1, 2012). Burglar returns family's stolen goods with
an apology note. Adds in $50 for broken door. *National Post*. https://
nationalpost.com/news/canada/guelph-police

Exline, J. J., & Baumeister, R. F. (2000). Expressing forgiveness and repent-
ance: Benefits and barriers. In M. E. McCullough, K. I. Pargament &
C. E. Thoresen (Eds.), *The psychology of forgiveness* (pp. 133–155).
Guilford.

Fehr, R., Gelfand, M. J., & Nag, M. (2010). The road to forgiveness: A
meta-analytic synthesis of its situational and dispositional correlates.
Psychological Bulletin, *136*(5), 894–914. https://doi.org/10.1037/
a0019993

Field, C., Zander, J., & Hall, G. (2013). 'Forgiveness is a present to yourself as well': An intrapersonal model of forgiveness in victims of violent
crime. *International Review of Victimology*, *19*(3), 235–247. https://doi.
org/10.1177/0269758013492752

Friedman, R., Anderson, C., Brett, J., Olekalns, M., Goates, N., &
Lisco, C. C. (2004). The positive and negative effects of anger on
dispute resolution: Evidence from electronically mediated disputes.
Journal of Applied Psychology, *89*(2), 369–376. https://doi.org/10.1037/
0021-9010.89.2.369

Funk, F., Walker, M., & Todorov, A. (2017). Modelling perceptions of
criminality and remorse from faces using a data-driven computational
approach. *Cognition and Emotion*, *31*(7), 1431–1443. https://doi.org/
10.1080/02699931.2016.1227305

Goffman, E. (1971). *Relations in public: Microstudies of the public order*.
Basic Books.

Graziano, W. G., & Eisenberg, N. (1997). Agreeableness: A dimension of
personality. In R. Hogan, J. Johnson, & S. Briggs (Eds.), *Handbook of
personality psychology* (pp. 795–824). Academic Press. https://doi.org/
10.1016/B978-012134645-4/50031-7

Greenwood, K. (2017, April 27). Dear governor, please don't execute the
man who murdered my father. *The Guardian.com*. www.theguardian.
com/commentisfree/2017/apr/27/dear-governor-please-dont-execute-
kennth-williams

Gruber, M. C. (2014). *"I'm sorry for what I've done": The language of
courtroom apologies*. Oxford.

Haidt, J. (2003). The moral emotions. In R. J. Davidson, K. R. Scherer, &
H. H. Goldsmith (Eds.), *Handbook of affective sciences* (pp. 852–870).
Oxford University Press.

Halmesvaara, O., Harjunen, V. J., Aulbach, M. B., & Ravaja, N. (2020). How bodily expressions of emotion after norm violation influence perceivers' moral judgments and prevent social exclusion: A socio-functional approach to nonverbal shame display. *PloS ONE, 15*(4), e0232298. https://doi.org/10.1371/journal.pone.0232298

Hand, C. A., Hankes, J., & House, T. (2012). Restorative justice: The indigenous justice system. *Contemporary Justice Review, 15*(4), 449–467. https://doi.org/10.1080/10282580.2012.734576

Haney, C., Sontag, L., & Constanzo, S. (1994). Deciding to take a life: Capital juries, sentencing instructions, and the jurisprudence of death. *Journal of Social Issues, 50*, 149–176. https://doi.org/10.1111/j.1540-4560.1994.tb02414.x

Hansen, T., & Umbreit, M. (2018). State of knowledge: Four decades of victim-offender mediation research and practice: The evidence. *Conflict Resolution Quarterly, 36*(2), 99–113. https://doi.org/10.1002/crq.21234

Heimreich, J. S. (2011). Does sorry incriminate? Evidence, harm and the protection of apology. *Cornell Journal of Law and Public Policy, 21*(3), 567–609.

Hille, P., Romaniec, R., & Bosen, R. (December 6, 2020). 50 years since Willy Brandt's historic gesture in Poland. *Deutsche Welle.* www.dw.com/en/germany-poland-reconciliation-willy-brandt/a-55828523

Hodgins, H. S., & Liebeskind, E. (2003). Apology versus defense: Antecedents and consequences. *Journal of Experimental Social Psychology, 39*, 297–316. https://doi.org/10.1016/S0022-1031(03)00024-6

Hornsey, M. J., Wohl, M. J. A., Harris, E. A., Okimoto, T. G., Thai, M., & Wenzel, M. (2020). Embodied remorse: Physical displays of remorse increase positive responses to public apologies, but have negligible effects on forgiveness. *Journal of Personality and Social Psychology, 119*(2), 367–389. https://doi.org/10.1037/pspi0000208

Karremans, J. C., Van Lange, P. A. M., Ouwerkerk, J. W., & Kluwer, E. S. (2003). When forgiving enhances psychological well-being: The role of interpersonal commitment. *Journal of Personality and Social Psychology, 84*(5), 1011–1026. https://doi.org/10.1037/0022-3514.84.5.1011

Kearns, J. N., & Fincham, F. D. (2004). A prototype analysis of forgiveness. *Personality and Social Psychology Bulletin, 30*(7), 838–855. https://doi.org/10.1177/0146167204264237

King, R. (2003). *Don't kill in our names: Families of murder victims speak out against the death penalty.* Rutgers University Press.

Lamb, S. (2002). Women, abuse and forgiveness: A special case. In S. Lamb & J. Murphy (Eds.), *Before forgiving: Cautioning views of forgiveness in psychotherapy* (pp. 155–171). Oxford University Press.

Lawler, K. A., Younger, J. W., Piferi, R. L., Jobe, R. L., Edmondson, K. A., & Jones, W. H. (2005). The unique effects of forgiveness on health: An exploration of pathways. *Journal of Behavioral Medicine, 28*(2), 157–167. https://doi.org/10.1007/s10865-005-3665-2

Luchies, L. B., Finkel, E. J., McNulty, J. K., & Kumashiro, M. (2010). The doormat effect: When forgiving erodes self-respect and self-concept clarity. *Journal of Personality and Social Psychology, 98*(5), 734–739. https://doi.org/10.1037/a0017838

Maltby, J., & Day, L. (2004). Forgiveness and defense style. *Journal of Genetic Psychology, 165*, 99–110. https://doi.org/10.3200/GNTP.165.1.99-112

McCart, M. R., Smith, D. W., & Sawyer, G. K. (2010). Help seeking among victims of crime: A review of the empirical literature. *Journal of Traumatic Stress: Official Publication of The International Society for Traumatic Stress Studies, 23*(2), 198–206. https://doi.org/10.1002/jts.20509

McCullough, M. E., Rachal, K. C., Sandage, S.J., Worthington, E.L., Jr., Brown, S.W., & Hight, T.L. (1998). Interpersonal forgiving in close relationships: II. Theoretical elaboration and measurement. *Journal of Personality and Social Psychology, 75*(6), 1586–1603. https://doi.org/10.1037/0022-3514.75.6.1586

McCullough, M. E., Worthington, E. L. J., & Rachal, K. C. (1997). Interpersonal forgiving in close relationships. *Journal of Personality and Social Psychology, 73*(2), 321–336. https://doi.org/10.1037/0022-3514.73.2.321

McNulty, J. K. (2010). Forgiveness increases the likelihood of subsequent partner transgressions in marriage. *Journal of Family Psychology, 24*, 787–790. https://doi.org/10.1037/a0021678

McNulty, J. K. (2011). The dark side of forgiveness: The tendency to forgive predicts continued psychological and physical aggression in marriage. *Personality and Social Psychology Bulletin, 37*(6), 770–783. https://doi.org/10.1177/0146167211407077

McNulty, J. K., & Russell, V. M. (2016). Forgive and forget, or forgive and regret? Whether forgiveness leads to less or more offending depends on offender agreeableness. *Personality and Social Psychology Bulletin, 42*(5), 616–631. https://doi.org/10.1177/0146167216637841

Murphy, J. G. (2000). Two cheers for vindictiveness. *Punishment & Society, 2(2)*, 131–143. https://doi.org/10.1177/14624740022227917

Murphy, J. G. (2007). Forgiveness, self-respect, and the value of resentment. In E. L. Worthington, Jr. (Ed.), *Handbook of forgiveness* (pp. 57–64). Routledge.

Ohtsubo, Y., Watanabe, E., Kim, J., Kulas, J. T., Muluk, H., Nazar, G., ... & Zhang, J. (2012). Are costly apologies universally perceived as being sincere? A test of the costly apology-perceived sincerity relationship in seven countries. *Journal of Evolutionary Psychology, 10*(4), 187–204. https://doi.org/10.1556/jep.10.2012.4.3

Petrucci, C. J. (2002). Apology in the criminal justice setting: Evidence for including apology as an additional component in the legal system.

Behavioral Sciences & the Law, 20(4), 337–362. https://doi.org/10.1002/bsl.495

Picó, A., Gračanin, A., Gadea, M., Boeren, A., Aliño, M., & Vingerhoets, A. (2020). How visible tears affect observers' judgements and behavioral intentions: Sincerity, remorse, and punishment. *Journal of Nonverbal Behavior, 44*(2), 215–232. https://doi.org/10.1007/s10919-019-00328-9

Proeve, M., & Tudor, S. (2016). *Remorse: Psychological and jurisprudential perspectives.* Routledge.

Restorative Justice International. (26 June, 2014). Apology banks: Good or bad? *Restorative Justice International.* www.restorativejusticeintern ational.com/apology-banks-good-or-bad/

Robbennolt, J. K. (2006). Apologies and settlement levers. *Journal of Empirical Legal Studies, 3*(2), 333–373. https://doi.org/10.1111/j.1740-1461.2006.00072.x

Rossmanith, K., Tudor, S., & Proeve, M. (2018). Courtroom contrition: How do judges know? *Griffith Law Review, 27*(3), 366–384. https://doi.org/10.1080/10383441.2018.1557588

Scher, S. J., & Darley, J. M. (1997). How effective are the things people say to apologize? Effects of the realization of the apology speech act. *Journal of Psycholinguistic Research, 26*, 127–140. http://dx.doi.org/10.1023/A:1025068306386

Shapland, J., Atkinson, A., Atkinson, H., Colledge, E., Dignan, J., Howes, M., ... & Sorsby, A. (2006). Situating restorative justice within criminal justice. *Theoretical Criminology, 10*(4), 505–532. https://doi.org/10.1177/1362480606068876

Sherman, L. W., Strang, H., Angel, C., Woods, D., Barnes, G. C., Bennett, S., & Inkpen, N. (2005). Effects of face-to-face restorative justice on victims of crime in four randomized, controlled trials. *Journal of Experimental Criminology, 1*, 367–395. https://doi.org/10.1007/s11 292-005-8126-y

Simons, M. A. (2004). Born again on death row: Retribution, remorse, and religion. *The Catholic Lawyer, 43*, 311–337.

Strang, H., & Sherman, L. W. (2003). Repairing the harm: Victims and restorative justice. *Utah Law Review, 15*, 15–42.

Strayer, F. F., & Trudel, M. (1984). Developmental changes in the nature and function of social dominance among young children. *Ethology and Sociobiology, 5*, 279–295. https://doi.org/10.1016/0162-3095(84)90007-4

Struthers, C. W., Eaton, J., Mendoza, R., Santelli, A. G., & Shirvani, N. (2010). Interrelationship among injured parties' attributions of responsibility, appraisal of appropriateness to forgive the transgressor, forgiveness, and repentance. *Journal of Applied Social Psychology, 40*(4), 970–1002. https://doi.org/10.1111/j.1559-1816.2010.00607.x

Struthers, C. W., Eaton, J., Shirvani, N., Georghiou, M., & Edell, E. (2008). The effect of preemptive forgiveness and a transgressor's responsibility on shame, motivation to reconcile, and repentance. *Basic and Applied Social Psychology, 30*(2), 130–141. https://doi.org/10.1080/0197353080 2209178

Tangney, J. P., Stuewig, J., & Hafez, L. (2011). Shame, guilt, and remorse: Implications for offender populations. *Journal of Forensic Psychiatry & Psychology, 22*(5), 706–723. https://doi.org/10.1080/14789 949.2011.617541

Tangney, J. P., Wagner, P., Fletcher, C., & Gramzow, R. (1992). Shamed into anger? The relation of shame and guilt to anger and self-reported aggression. *Journal of Personality and Social Psychology, 62*(4), 669–675. https://doi.org/10.1037/0022-3514.62.4.669

Tavuchis, N. (1991). *Mea culpa: A sociology of apology and reconciliation.* Stanford University Press.

ten Brinke, L., & Adams, G. S. (2015). Saving face? When emotion displays during public apologies mitigate damage to organizational performance. *Organizational Behavior and Human Decision Processes, 130*, 1–12. https://doi.org/10.1016/j.obhdp.2015.05.003

Tittler, M. V., & Wade, N. G. (2019). Forgiveness interventions from a multicultural perspective: Potential applications and concerns. In L. E. Van Zyl & S. Rothmann Sr. (Eds.), *Theoretical approaches to multicultural positive psychological interventions* (pp. 179–199). Springer. https://doi.org/10.1007/978-3-030-20583-6_8

Tudor, S., Weisman, R., Proeve, M, & Rossmanith, K. (Eds.). (2022). *Remorse and criminal justice: Multi-disciplinary perspectives.* Routledge.

Umbreit, M. S. (1994). *Victim meets offender: The impact of restorative justice and mediation.* Willow Tree Press.

Umbreit, M. S., & Armour, M. P. (2010). *Restorative justice dialogue: An essential guide for research and practice.* Springer.

Umbreit, M. S., Bradshaw, W., & Coates, R. B. (1999). Victims of severe violence meet the offender: Restorative justice through dialogue. *International Review of Victimology, 6*, 321–343. https://doi.org/10.1177/026975809900600405

Umbreit, M. S., & Vos, B. (2000). Homicide survivors meet the offender prior to execution: Restorative justice through dialogue. *Homicide Studies, 4*(1), 63–87. https://doi.org/10.1177/1088767900004001004

VanItallie, T. B. (2002). Stress: A risk factor for serious illness. *Metabolism, 51*, 40–45. https://doi.org/10.1053/meta.2002.33191

Weisman, R. (2004). Showing remorse: Reflections on the gap between expression and attribution in cases of wrongful conviction. *Canadian Journal of Criminology and Criminal Justice, 46*(2), 121–138. https://doi.org/10.3138/cjccj.46.2.121

Weisman, R. (2009) Being and doing: The judicial use of remorse to construct character and community. *Social & Legal Studies, 18*(1): 47–69. https://doi.org/10.1177/0964663908100333

Witvliet, C., Ludwig, T. E., & Vander Laan, K. L. (2001). Granting forgiveness or harboring grudges: Implications for emotion, physiology, and health. *Psychological Science, 12*, 117–123. https://doi.org/10.1111/1467-9280.00320

Witvliet, C. V. O., Wade, N. G., Worthington, E. L., Jr. Root Luna, L., Van Tongeren, D. R., Berry, J. W., & Tsang, J-A. (2020). Apology and restitution: Offender accountability responses influence victim empathy and forgiveness. *Journal of Psychology and Theology, 48*(2), 88–104. https://doi.org/10.1177/0091647120915181

Worthington, E. L., & Scherer, M. (2004). Forgiveness is an emotion-focused coping strategy that can reduce health risks and promote health resilience: Theory, review, and hypotheses. *Psychology & Health, 19*(3), 385–405. https://doi.org/10.1080/0887044042000196674

Ysseldyk, R., Matheson, K., & Anisman, H. (2007). Rumination: Bridging a gap between forgiving, vengefulness, and psychological health. *Personality and Individual Differences, 42*(8), 1573–1584. https://doi.org/10.1016/j.paid.2006.10.032

Zehr, H. (2015). *The little book of restorative justice: Revised and updated.* Simon and Schuster.

Zehr, H., & Mika, H. (2017). Fundamental concepts of restorative justice. In D. Roche (Ed.), *Restorative Justice* (pp. 73–81). Routledge.

2 Remorse in the unique context of death row

Chapter 1 made the argument that apology and forgiveness have a place in criminal justice. When offenders feel remorse and victims have the opportunity to learn of this remorse, both parties can benefit. Even though much of the research on how and why apologies can lead to forgiveness – and the conditions under which they do not – comes from research in psychology and sociology that focuses on non-criminal transgressions and offences, the underlying mechanisms are relevant in criminal offences too. While criminal offences are clearly different from interpersonal offences, they still involve an offence, albeit one that violates the rule of law. Is there a limit, however, to how severe the offence can be before our general understanding of apologies and forgiveness do not apply? Can we assume that the same processes occur when the offence committed is homicide and the offender is facing a death sentence?

This chapter considers the idea of remorse in inmates who are on death row. It begins with an overview of capital punishment, first globally and then specifically in the United States. It then explores the complex issue of whether inmates on death row are capable of remorse, and, if they are, what this remorse might look like.

Capital punishment – a brief history

Capital punishment, also known as the death penalty, has a long history. Evidence of humans killing other humans as punishment for their misdeeds can be found in most societies throughout

DOI: 10.4324/9781003384946-2

history. One of the earliest recorded death sentences was in Egypt in the 16th century BCE, where a member of the Egyptian nobility was ordered to take his own life for allegedly performing magic (Laurence, 1960). The first known mention of capital punishment as a formal law dates back to the 18th century BCE, in the Code of Hammurabi. The Code of Hammurabi is a set of 282 laws and rules enacted by the Babylonian king Hammurabi and inscribed on a stone pillar. The code established a system of justice that provided fair punishments that were proportional to the crime committed. As such, it lists the death penalty as punishment for 25 different crimes (Randa, 1997). The term "capital punishment" comes from the Latin word *caput*, which means head, referencing the fact that a common means of execution was beheading, or decapitation (Kronenwetter, 2001). In addition to beheading, there are historical records of executions by methods such as hanging, stoning, drowning, poisoning, burning at the stake, starvation, and burying alive (Laurence, 1960). More modern methods include firing squad, the electric chair, and lethal injection.

Historically, death sentences have been imposed for a variety of crimes, ranging from very minor offences like stealing to more severe offences like murder. Over time, the offences that are punishable by death have generally been reduced to only the most severe crimes, such as murder and crimes against the state, although this is not true of all countries that still have the death penalty. For example, in Saudi Arabia one can still be executed for witchcraft and sorcery (ECDHR, 2023), and China's criminal law lists the death penalty as punishment for acts such as arson, destroying a vehicle, and robbery (China Justice Observer, 2020). Amnesty International (2022) reported that in 2021 individuals were executed for drug-related offences (e.g., China, Egypt, Malaysia), financial corruption (e.g., Iran), protesting (e.g., Saudi Arabia), igniting wildfires (e.g., Syria), and violent crimes committed by foreign nationals (e.g., United Arab Emirates), in addition to murder.

According to Amnesty International (2023), 52 countries around the world still have the death penalty. Amnesty reports that an estimated 883 individuals were executed in 20 different countries in 2022, although the actual number is likely much higher because some countries do not make this information available. China had the highest number of known executions, followed by Iran, Egypt, Saudi Arabia, and Syria.

Public support for capital punishment has been declining steadily, and so has the number of countries that have it as part of their laws. The United Kingdom abolished the death penalty in 1965, followed by Canada in 1976 and Australia in 1985. Protocol 13 of the European Convention on Human Rights abolished it in 2002 for all members of the European Union, although many members had already abolished it. More recently, Sierra Leone and Kazakhstan abolished it in 2021 and Papua New Guinea, the Central African Republic, Equatorial Guinea, and Zambia abolished it in 2022 (Amnesty International, 2023).

Capital punishment in the United States

History

The United States is the only developed Western democracy to still have the death penalty (Steiker & Steiker, 2020). It is not united in its support of capital punishment: As of summer 2023, only 27 states still have the death penalty. In fact, some US states have been remarkably progressive in limiting their use of the death penalty. In 1794 the state of Pennsylvania was among the first in the world to restrict capital punishment to cases of first-degree murder; Germany, England, and Wales followed suit in the 1800s (Hood & Hoyle, 2015). The United States is unique among countries that still have capital punishment because it tends to keep detailed records of its executions. Data are available on all executions performed in the United States from the year 1608 until the present. Although the older data (compiled by Espy and Smykla, 2016) includes only the main details, such as the age and race of the offender, the nature of the crime, and the method of execution, more recent data includes many details about the process, including information about the victims, the legal proceedings, the offenders' last words, and even, in some cases, what they ate for their last meal. Because each state has its own laws and processes around capital punishment, there is less consistency in terms of what and how the information is shared.

The first recorded execution in the United States (at that time known as the British North American Colonies) took place in Virginia, in 1608. Captain George Kendall was executed by firing squad after being accused of being a spy (Stein, 2017). The next recorded execution in the United States wasn't until 1622 (Daniell Frank, who was hanged in Virginia for theft). The number of executions increased slowly but steadily over time, until it reached a peak in 1937, with 197 executions that year. The states with the most executions since record keeping began are Virginia (with 1387 executions), New York (1130 executions), Pennsylvania (1043 executions), and Texas (1320 executions) (Death Penalty Information Centre, 2023a; Espy & Smykla, 2016). These numbers do not tell the entire story, however, because they are simply the total number of individuals executed in the state and not per capita numbers. The populations of these states have grown at different rates, so higher numbers might just reflect a higher population rather than a higher rate of executions in that state. Another issue to take into consideration is that the numbers are not directly comparable because these states did not all become part of the United States at the same time. For example, Texas became a state later than Virginia, New York, and Pennsylvania, so its executions have taken place over a shorter period of time than the other states.

Each of the US states has its own laws regarding capital punishment, and executions can also occur at the federal level. Federal executions tend to be (although are not always) for more serious crimes. For example, Timothy McVeigh, who bombed a government building in Oklahoma in 1995, killing 168 people, was executed at the federal level. Although officially 27 states still have the death penalty, some of them haven't executed anyone for more than 10 years, and some of them have governor-imposed moratoriums. This means that less than half of the states with the death penalty are currently engaging in executions (Death Penalty Information Centre, 2023b).

There was a brief period where executions were halted across the United States. In 1972, William Henry Furman was sentenced to death in Georgia for killing a homeowner during a robbery. He appealed the decision, and the Supreme Court, when considering Furman's case along with the cases of two other Black men who had also been sentenced to death, reversed their sentences and ruled that the death penalty was unconstitutional because it unfairly targeted socially disadvantaged individuals. This resulted in a moratorium on the death penalty until 1976, when the ruling was repealed and the states began handing out death sentences again (Stein, 2017). US historians refer to capital punishment after this case as the "post-Furman" era, or the "modern" era. After the Furman case, the number of executions in the US remained low until the 1980s, until it reached a peak of 98 executions in 1999. The number has been steadily declining since then, with an average of approximately 20 per year since 2016. Of the 1571 executions carried out in the post-Furman era (as of Summer 2023), 583 of them have been in Texas (Death Penalty Information Centre, 2023a).

Public opinion

Americans tend to be divided in their opinions on capital punishment, although more are in favour of it than opposed to it. When asked in a 2022 opinion poll whether they agreed with the death penalty as a punishment for those who have committed murder, 55% were in favour and 42% were opposed, with the rest being undecided (Gallup, 2023). A more detailed assessment of public opinion from 2021 indicated that there is some nuance to these opinions. In this poll, of the 59% who favoured the death penalty for persons convicted of murder, 27% indicated that they "strongly" favoured it and 32% indicated that they "somewhat" favoured it, and amongst the 39% who opposed it, 24% "somewhat" opposed it and only 15% "strongly" opposed it. The remaining 2% did not answer the question (Pew Research Centre, 2021). The higher percentages of people who chose "somewhat" over "strongly" suggests that opinions on the death penalty are not necessarily as extreme as a "yes" or "no" answer might imply. This also means that those who hold less extreme attitudes towards the death penalty might be more willing to change their mind.

While they may not be extreme in their opinions, Americans have been fairly consistent. Yearly Gallup polls dating back to 1937 (Gallup, 2023) show that support of the death penalty has always been higher than opposition to it, with the exception of 1966, when opposition reached 47%, compared to only 42% support. Support for the death penalty reached a peak in 1994, at 80%, but has gradually diminished since then. When asked about their reasons for supporting the death penalty, the most common reason mentioned by Americans was that the punishment fits the crime, or that the offender deserved it (Gallup, 2023). They also mention, in order of importance, the costs associated with keeping someone in prison for life, the death penalty serving as a deterrent to other potential offenders, the low chance of rehabilitation of the offender, and the fact that it would help the families of the victims. This concern for victims is reflected in a poll by the *Washington Post* (2001), in which 60% of respondents agreed with the statement, "The death penalty is fair because it gives satisfaction and closure to the families of murder victims."

Racism and other bias in sentencing decisions

The reason for the pause in capital punishment in 1972 was that sentencing decisions were seen as being arbitrary and biased. Juries were generally not provided with guidance on how to decide whether to recommend the death penalty or not, and their recommendations were sometimes inconsistent and biased against those who were Black, uneducated, and poor, and/or mentally ill (Bright, 2014). When the death penalty was reintroduced in 1976 it was with more clear guidelines on what constitutes aggravating and mitigating factors (Lynch & Haney, 2000). In the 1990s, researchers interviewed between 80 and 120 jurors from each of 14 different states to assess whether these guidelines had any effect on bias in sentencing decisions (Bowers, 1995). This far-ranging study, called the Capital Jury Project, concluded that racial bias had not disappeared from the system, and that it was most pronounced when white jurors made decisions about crimes involving Black defendants and white victims (Bowers et al., 2001). More recent research has found that this bias against Black defendants continues (Alesina & La Ferrara, 2014; Hoag, 2020). This bias is not specific to the death penalty. Structural inequality and racism affect many aspects of the justice system, including policing, jury selection, and post-sentencing decisions, and it is likely that these biases are manifest in capital cases as well (Phillips & Marceau, 2020).

Poverty is also a risk factor for ending up on death row. This is due to both structural inequalities and the fact that those who can afford competent legal representation are more likely to avoid a death penalty. Poor defendants who cannot afford their own lawyer are appointed one, but these court-appointed lawyers might not be trained to work on capital cases, they might be underpaid/overworked, or they might not have adequate resources to adequately defend their client (Bright, 2014).

Those with diminished mental capacity have also experienced bias in capital cases. An individual with an intellectual disability might not be able to understand or follow the law or they might be more likely to give a false confession, which would make them more likely to be falsely convicted. Although there are now more stringent requirements in place to determine whether a defendant has the mental capacity to understand the implications of their crime, the way that these requirements are interpreted and implemented varies across jurisdictions, and some defendants who meet the criteria for an intellectual disability are given death sentences anyway (Blume et al., 2014). There are also biases within the system against those who are mentally ill. Efforts to label some offenders as psychopathic or as having underlying neurological causes for their behaviour, instead of convincing juries that they are not criminally responsible, can make them more likely to be given a death sentence because juries assume that they are less likely to respond to treatment and are thus unredeemable (Edens et al., 2005; Pyun, 2015).

The execution process

The US states that still have the death penalty have different laws regarding how it is applied, what crimes are eligible for it, and how it is carried out. The basic process from original conviction to execution can be long and involved, with multiple opportunities for the offender to appeal the sentence. Even when their avenues for appeal have been exhausted they can still ask for clemency from the state governor. This process takes time, and offenders spend an average of more than ten years on death row before they are executed. If they waive their right to appeal the time can be much shorter. The Texas Department of Criminal Justice (2023) reports times on death row as short as 252 days (Joe Gonzales, executed in 1999) and as long as 11,575 days (31 years; David Lee Powell, executed in 2010).

Procedures for the execution itself have changed significantly since the days of public hangings, where it was believed that allowing the general public to witness the gruesome nature of an execution first-hand might serve as a deterrent. Evidence to support this assumption is weak, however, as examinations of historical crime rates have shown, homicides actually tended to increase in the days and weeks following public executions (Bowers & Pierce, 1980). Rather than discouraging people from committing similar crimes, the public executions seemed to send the message that if it was okay for the state to kill people, then it was okay for everyone else to as well. Public executions tended to be very well-attended, raucous affairs, with lots of public drunkenness, fighting, and, ironically, crime (Madow, 1995). After witnessing a public hanging in London in 1849, Charles Dickens wrote a letter to the *Times*, denouncing what he called the "brutal mirth" of the spectators:

> I believe that a sight so inconceivably awful as the wickedness and levity of the immense crowd collected at that execution this morning could be imagined by no man, and could be presented in no heathen land under the sun. The horrors of the gibbet and of the crime which brought the wretched murderers to it faded in my mind before the atrocious bearing, looks, and language of the assembled spectators.
>
> (Dickens, 1849)

By the 20th century almost all of the states had made executions private, amidst concerns that their public nature was serving as entertainment rather than deterrence. In 1936, Kentucky held the last public execution in the United States, attended by as many as 20,000 spectators. The press reported more on the behaviour of the crowd and the carnival-like atmosphere than the execution itself, with reports of people tearing off parts of the execution hood for souvenirs (Banner, 2002). After this, executions were moved to the prisons, with only pre-approved spectators permitted. As attitudes and executions methods changed, with smaller execution chambers and less of an appetite for spectacle, the only people permitted to witness the execution were members of the press and a small number of the offender's family and friends. More recently, in response to campaigns by survivors and victim's rights advocates, the states began allowing the family and close friends of victim's family to witness executions as well.

While specific protocols vary between the states, the execution process is standardized. Typically, the offender is put on a death watch before the execution, and often they are moved to a different location. Some jurisdictions allow them to request a special meal the day before the execution. During this time the inmate has the opportunity to meet with religious/spiritual advisors, their family, and sometimes, with special permission, the press. On the day of the execution they are taken to the execution chamber, which is typically a small room with a window (in some cases a one-way mirror) and a microphone. Some prisons, including the one in Texas where executions take place, have two witness rooms: one for the offender's family and one for the victim's family. They cannot see the offender until the preparation for the lethal injection has been completed. Once these preparations are complete, the curtains are opened and the witnesses can see the inmate. The offender is given the opportunity to make a final statement, after which they are injected with the lethal chemicals and pronounced dead. The Texas Department of Criminal Justice (2023) reports that the viewing process takes between seven and ten minutes.

Rules about who is permitted to witness an execution vary by state, but generally the witnesses may include official witnesses (correctional officers, medical personnel, and representatives of the state or federal government), offender witnesses (family and friends of the offender, a spiritual advisor), victim witnesses (family and friends of the victim(s)), and media witnesses. The number of witnesses permitted is typically limited, and there are strict rules about protocol. Background checks may be required, and attendees may be limited as to what they can take into the room. In some jurisdictions (for example, Texas), the victim witnesses arrive at the prison early, for additional support and preparation, and are taken to a separate room to debrief after the execution. Witnesses may hold a formal press conference or speak informally with the media upon leaving the prison.

The last statement

One courtesy offered to inmates before they are executed is the opportunity to make a last statement. This is a longstanding tradition in executions, dating back at least as far as the 17th century (LaChance, 2007). In these "gallows speeches," as they were called, the condemned prisoners were encouraged to admit to their crimes and acknowledge their criminal past, to both serve as a warning to those gathered to watch the execution and to legitimize the severity of the punishment. Some went off-script, however, and used the opportunity to claim innocence, blame others, or criticize the judicial system (Banner, 2002). Sometimes their final words were printed in a pamphlet, with details of their crime, the trial, and the execution. These pamphlets, which tended to include gory details of the execution and sometimes even an illustration or photo of the execution, were widely distributed and very popular, making the spectacle of the execution available to a much larger audience (Guthke, 1992).

Although they are no longer referred to as "gallows speeches," in the United States the final words of executed inmates are still recorded and shared with the public. The modern version of these execution pamphlets is the newspaper article, written by the members of the press who have been invited to witness the execution. They do not provide gory details or photos, but they do serve as a public record of the event. They also may include all or part of the final words of the inmate. While some state justice departments, notably that of Texas, also document the final words and make them available on their website, others either do not record them or do not make them publicly available.

Capital punishment and remorse

When an individual is tried for capital murder there are typically two significant decisions that must be made: (1) whether the person is guilty, and, if they are found to be guilty, (2) whether they deserve the death penalty or life in prison. Just being found guilty of murder is not enough to warrant the death penalty; the jury or judge must also consider whether there are mitigating factors. For example, if the offender has no criminal history, or they were mentally or emotionally distressed at the time of the crime, or they did not have the mental capacity to understand the implications of their actions, then the jury can recommend life in prison instead of a death sentence (Cheng, 2010). Another factor that is taken into consideration when making sentencing decisions is remorse. Jurors are more likely to recommend the death penalty when they believe that the offender lacks remorse (Haney et al., 1994; Costanzo & Costanzo, 1992; Sundby, 1998).

Lack of remorse or an offender's failure to acknowledge or understand the harm they have caused leads others to believe that they will not change their behaviour and that they are, therefore, less deserving of mercy (Murphy, 2007). Surveys of public attitudes towards crime show that the less redeemable an offender is judged to be, the harsher the punishment they are considered to deserve (Burton et al., 2020; Maruna & King, 2009). Lack of remorse may suggest that the individual poses a threat to the social order. An individual who is truly remorseful feels guilt and shame for their actions and fully understands and acknowledges that they have violated a social code (Bandes, 2014; Murphy, 2006). Maintaining social order depends on everyone understanding and obeying not only the formal rules of society but also the unwritten norms of behaviour. The formal rules of society specify that we do not kill each other, and the informal code specifies, for example, that we treat each other kindly and that we show remorse when we fail to maintain the social order. When an offender is remorseful, they are demonstrating that they understand and share society's formal and informal norms and values and that they are committed to uphold them. Remorse indicates that the offender will not repeat the harmful act, and therefore that they have the capacity for redemption. Murphy (2007) quotes a decision made to deny clemency to Stanley "Tookie" Williams on the grounds that Williams, who maintained that he was innocent, refused to apologize:

> Without an apology and atonement for these senseless and brutal killings there can be no redemption. In this case, the one thing that would be the clearest indication of complete remorse and full redemption is the one thing Williams will not do.
>
> (p. 424)

The assumed connection between remorse and potential redeemability means that, in some cases, life and death decisions are based on whether the accused appears to be remorseful. As discussed in Chapter 1, true remorse can be difficult to identify or label because it is largely an internal process. Jurors in capital cases must decode verbal and non-verbal cues, often without context or even a clear definition of what remorse actually is (Bandes, 2016). They might be unaware of cultural differences in displays of remorse (Everett & Nienstedt, 1999), or they might have racial biases that cause them to misidentify remorse in specific groups (Bowers et al., 2001). They might be sceptical about an offender claiming to be remorseful, especially if they believe the offender had been encouraged to do so by their legal counsel. The fact that jury decisions about remorse are fallible calls into question the idea that the death penalty is reserved for those who are unredeemable. There are many moral and ethical questions about capital punishment, most of which are beyond the scope of this book, but one important question to raise here is whether individuals who have been sentenced to death actually *are* remorseful.

Clearly there is not one single answer to this question. The remainder of this chapter explores some of the challenges of remorse in the context of capital punishment. It addresses why it can be difficult to see those on death row as even being capable of remorse, why it might be difficult for those who are remorseful to convince others of that that they are, and why some might, indeed, be unremorseful.

Are death row offenders capable of remorse?

Typically, when one individual commits a transgression against another individual, a sincere expression of remorse can repair the damage and help reconcile those involved. If the harm-doer acknowledges the harm done, takes responsibility for it, offers an apology, and promises not to repeat the offence, then the harmed person will likely forgive them. While this process of remorse and forgiveness is relatively straightforward in the context of interpersonal transgressions, it becomes more complex when the transgression is an actual crime. It can be much more difficult for a criminal offender to both show remorse and convince others that this remorse is sincere. These challenges are further compounded when the criminal offence is particularly serious, such as when the offender is charged with capital murder and sentenced to death. The serious nature of the crime makes the need for remorse even more salient but, ironically, it also makes the offender's remorse less likely to be seen as sincere or authentic (Murphy, 2006).

One reason for this is that serious offenders are often viewed as being qualitatively different from non-offenders. These attitudes date back to the theories of Cesare Lombroso in the late 1800s, who proposed that criminals were physiologically different from non-criminals. He claimed to be able to identify criminals by their physical features (Lombroso-Ferrero, 1911). Lombroso concluded that these differences indicated that criminals were less evolved, or more primitive, than non-criminals and thus were not capable of the kind of higher-level moral reasoning that would be required to feel remorse. This "criminology of the other" (Garland, 2001, p. 136) results in criminal offenders being perceived as somehow less than human (e.g., Vandiver et al., 2002; Vasiljevic & Viki, 2013) or, at the very least, unredeemable (e.g., Edens et al., 2013). When they are presented in the media they tend to be described solely in terms of the crimes they committed rather than by the social context that might have led to those crimes (Haney, 1995). This helps perpetuate stereotypes of people on death row as being monsters who are far enough outside of the social order to justify not expending resources to help rehabilitate them.

This dehumanizing of offenders not only helps to justify their inhumane treatment by the criminal justice system, but it also makes it difficult to view them as capable of understanding and following the moral codes of society. If one assumes that death row offenders do not have an understanding of the moral codes they have broken, then one would also conclude that these offenders are incapable of feeling remorse for their actions (Vasiljevic & Viki, 2013).

The challenges of showing remorse

Making a sincere apology is hard, even when the offence is relatively minor. People on death row have been convicted of a capital crime, which typically means first-degree murder in addition to some other aggravating factor such as sexual assault or armed robbery or the murder of a police officer or other justice professional (Davis & Snell, 2018). While it would certainly be possible to regret and feel true remorse for these actions, taking full responsibility for it would mean admitting to yourself and others that you violated one of the most universal moral codes: to not harm others (Kinnier et al., 2000). To be able to do this while also managing the threat and uncertainty of a death sentence, or the possibility of one, is unimaginable.

One factor contributing to the difficulty of showing remorse is the context in which offenders must do it. Typically, the last chance offenders have to alter their sentence by showing remorse is during their trial. They must convince a jury that they are truly remorseful, and they must do it in a public courtroom. While the offender's legal counsel will be there to support them and they may have family and friends present, others in the courtroom may be either indifferent or hostile to their plight. Family and loved ones of the victim may wish to see the offender receive the maximum punishment for their crime. This might make it very difficult for the offender to authentically demonstrate their remorse. Fear of public speaking is the most common social phobia (Ruscio et al., 2008). Even when the audience is sympathetic and engaged, imagine doing it in front of a group of people who may be angry, grieving, and/or vengeful because of your direct actions.

Another factor contributing to this stress is the fact that the offender may lack the skills needed to make an articulate and cohesive apology. Advanced academic training is not required to be remorseful, but to convince others of your remorse requires basic literacy skills. In 2019, almost half of offenders on death row did not have a high school education, and 12% had an eighth-grade education or less (Snell, 2021). Individuals with intellectual disabilities and those with serious mental illness might also struggle with expressing their remorse. Although there are laws in place to prevent the execution of individuals with intellectual disabilities, the proportion of inmates with cognitive deficiencies is higher in prisons than in the general population (Miley et al., 2020; Mogavero, 2020). In addition to not being able to articulate their remorse, those with mental health or cognitive challenges might not understand the ramification of their actions and thus would not be aware that they should feel remorse. They also might not feel remorse because they did not commit the crime they are being accused of. Individuals with cognitive deficiencies or a serious mental illness such as schizophrenia are more susceptible to making false confessions, leading to wrongful convictions that could result in them being given a capital sentence (Carl, 2020).

An additional factor that might limit the expression of remorse by a person accused of a capital crime is that, in addition to the fear and uncertainty they must be experiencing, they might also feel betrayed and angry at a justice system that they believe is unfair. Individuals accused of capital crimes might have legitimate reasons to feel this way: The system tends to discriminate against certain individuals, especially those who are Black, Hispanic, or poor. Racism within the justice system is well documented. People of colour are more likely to be stopped by police, arrested, and charged with a crime (Murakawa, 2019); they are often tried in courts with all-white lawyers, judges, and juries (Bright, 2014); and they are more likely to receive the death penalty, especially if the victim was white (Bowers et al., 2001). Individuals accused of capital crimes are also likely to have poor legal representation. Remorse might not be the primary concern of individuals who feel unduly targeted because of factors outside of their control.

Why death row offenders might not be remorseful

Some individuals on death row do not feel remorse for their crimes. One obvious and particularly unsettling reason for this might be because they are not guilty. The justice system is not perfect, and innocent people are sometimes sentenced to death. According to the Death Penalty Information Centre (2023c), as of May 2023, a total of 192 people on death row have been exonerated, which means that they were found not guilty of the charges that lead to their capital sentence. Few resources are typically put towards clearing the names of those who have already been executed, but the Death Penalty Information Centre estimates that at least 20 people who have been executed were likely innocent. While exact numbers are impossible to determine, it is estimated that at least 4.1% of inmates on currently on death row are innocent (Gross et al., 2014).

Innocent people charged with a capital crime are in a very diffi-cult position. If they profess their innocence they will perceived as lacking in remorse. As Weisman (2014) notes:

> It is important to note that the person who claims innocence is attributed all of the most damning characteristics of the remorseless offender – utter indifference to the suffering of their victim, lack of accountability for their actions, and no display of feeling in a circumstance where such feelings are expected from a member of the moral community.
>
> (p. 92)

If they do not show remorse (because they have nothing to be remorseful for) then they are more likely to be given a death sen-tence, but if they try to show remorse and it is not perceived as genuine (because their remorse is fake) then they may also receive a death sentence.

There are other reasons why offenders might not show remorse. Even if they do not believe they are innocent, some may have felt justified in their actions if, for example, they claimed that they acted in self-defence. This is probably a relatively small subset of individuals on death row, however, since providing evidence of self-defence likely would have saved them from the death penalty. Others may not feel remorse because they do not feel responsible for the crime – if they claimed that someone paid them to commit the crime, for example. It's also possible that some may simply have no regrets.

It is also possible that some offenders might be incapable of feeling remorse. In an early study of criminal behaviour, Cleckley (1941) identified a subset of individuals who were high functioning in most ways but tended to be manipulative, impulsive, and lacking in basic emotional responses like empathy and remorse. He called this the "psychopathic personality." Modern definitions of psychopathy build on this conceptualization, defining it as a clinical disorder characterized by "egocentricity, pathological lying, and manipulativeness; shallow emotions as well as lack of empathy, guilt, and remorse; impulsivity and irresponsibility; and a range of unethical and antisocial behaviours, not necessarily criminal" (Baglole et al., 2022, p. 535). It is estimated that the prevalence of psychopathy in the general population is less than 1%, while its prevalence in the prison population is approximately 25% (Hare, 1996). A typical score on the Revised Psychopathy Checklist (PCL-R; Hare, 1991) for those who are not criminal offenders is 5, while homicide offenders score an average of 21.2 (Fox & DeLisi, 2019). The small amount of research that has looked at prevalence rates in capital cases has found that approximately one-third of death row inmates meet the clinical criteria for a diagnosis of psychopathy (DeLisi et al., 2023). It is likely, then, that at least some individuals on death row are incapable of feeling remorse.

Although there is little doubt that the characteristics of a person with psychopathy are similar to many of the characteristics we associate with people who commit crimes – deceitfulness, impulsivity, and a lack of empathy and remorse – the fact that only one-third of inmates on death row meet the criteria for a clinical diagnosis for psychopathy means that two-thirds of offenders on death row are not psychopaths and hence may be capable of remorse. This is contrary to public perceptions of the death row offender. In part due to the media portrayals of psychopaths such as Ted Bundy and Charles Manson, people often assume that all inmates on death row are similarly cold-hearted and incapable of remorse (Edens et al., 2013). This connection, unfortunately, can be circular: Offenders who do not appear to be remorseful at their trials are more likely to be assumed to be psychopaths and thus sentenced to death (Edens et al., 2013), and once they are sentenced to death they are assumed to be psychopaths incapable of remorse.

Evidence of remorseful death row offenders

When judges and juries have difficulty identifying genuine remorse and offenders might be encouraged to fake remorse in order to reduce their sentence, how do we know if anyone accused of a capital crime is remorseful? Those who were able to effectively convince others of their remorse would have had a better chance of avoiding a death sentence, which leaves the question of whether individuals on death row are unremorseful or whether they were simply not able to successfully demonstrate their remorse.

Death row contains a diverse mix of individuals, and the answer to this question is probably that some of them are remorseful and some of them are not. Research on the emotional lives of inmates on death row is sparse, so there is very little data that could help answer this question. The research that does exist tends to be either from interviews with jurors and judges regarding their perceptions of offenders' remorse during the trial state or interviews with individual offenders while they are on death row.

Juror perceptions of offender remorse

As stated above, offenders who receive a death penalty are generally not perceived as being remorseful or else they likely would have received a lighter sentence (i.e., life in prison). In looking specifically at the California data from the Capital Jury Project, Sundby (1998) found only 2 of the defendants in 37 different trials were deemed to be remorseful by juries and given a life sentence instead of the death penalty. In a study assessing the data from South Carolina juries perceived similarly low rates of remorse in capital offenders (Eisenberg et al., 1998). Both studies found that juries were significantly more likely to recommend life in prison over a death sentence when they believed that the defendant was remorseful. In examining individual juror responses to the question, "When you were considering the punishment, did you believe that the defendant was truly sorry for the crime?" 9% of jurors in cases that ultimately decided on the death penalty indicated some degree of agreement (they either chose "Yes, sure he was sorry" or "Yes, I think he was sorry") (Sundby, 1998, p. 1569). This number suggests that, while some offenders might be perceived as remorseful by some jury members, it appears to be rare.

Although most jurors found no evidence of remorse in capital defendants, the fact that 9% of jurors did see them as remorseful is not trivial – it means that there is a certain degree of subjectivity in this area. In many cases the defendant does not testify, so jurors must base their judgments on how the defendant looks during the trial. In their interviews for the Capital Jury Project, jurors noted that defendants seemed remorseless because they "showed no emotion," were "bored and indifferent to the whole thing," "never made eye contact with the jury," or were "cocky, disruptive, clever, smart, calculating" (Sundby, 1998, pp. 1563–1564). While some of these behaviours might be accurately interpreted as a lack of remorse, they may also be the result of the defendant being instructed by their legal counsel to not show emotion or to not engage with the jurors. They might also be the result of the defendant deliberately trying to mask their own pain and pretend that they were not affected by the harm they had done (Ross, 2007).

There are also other factors that might influence jury perceptions of remorse. For instance, the more heinous the crime, the less likely the jurors are to see the defendant as remorseful. In addition, the more jurors support the death penalty, the less likely they are to see the defendant as remorseful (Eisenberg et al., 1998). The prosecutors also can influence the jury, and often refer to the defendant's apparent lack of remorse in their closing arguments (Sundby, 1998). While the number of defendants who show evidence of remorse while on trial may be low, it also seems likely that juries are not well-trained to identify true remorse even if offenders are able to demonstrate it in the confines of the courtroom.

Remorse during incarceration

Just because they might not have felt remorseful during the trial, it is possible for offenders to develop feelings of remorse while they are on death row. One of the most well-known cases of an offender's transformation while on death row is Karla Faye Tucker, who was sentenced to death for her role in the grisly murder of two people in Houston, Texas in 1983. Not long after she was arrested and awaiting trial, Tucker converted to Christianity and spend the rest of her time in prison counselling other inmates and helping their families. She married the prison chaplain and was highly respected by the guards (Sigler, 2006). She connected with Ron Carlson, the brother of one of her victims, and expressed her remorse in a letter to him:

> I have shared my heart with you and said I'm sorry, and I'll say it as many times as you need to hear it…I wish I could take it all back.
>
> (King, 2003, p. 76)

Ron forgave Tucker and campaigned, along with many other supporters, to commute her sentence to life in prison. There was widespread belief, among her legal team, the prison guards, and others who knew her, that she had been transformed by her remorse into a completely different person and that she was no longer at all similar to the person who had committed the murders (Long, 1999; Sigler, 2006). George W. Bush, who was the governor of Texas at the time, refused to commute her sentence, and she was executed in 1998.

There are other, less publicized, cases of inmates on death row who expressed their remorse to the families of their victims. Umbreit and Vos (2000) describe two cases of victim–offender mediation, where arrangements were made for the inmates and the covictims to meet. Both inmates agreed to the mediation because they wanted to apologize, and both reported feeling satisfied with the outcome because they felt that they had been able to do something positive to help the covictims heal. Offenders sometimes express their remorse in letters if mediation is not possible, and while covictims' responses to these letters tend to be mixed, regardless of whether they forgive the offender or not they do sometimes acknowledge that the offender showed remorse (Barrile, 2015). Other offenders have written about their remorse but have not had the opportunity to express it directly to the victims (Ross, 2007).

Sometimes the development of remorse while on death row is, as in the case of Karla Tucker, a result of religious conversion. Although a religious conversion does not always mean that one is remorseful (Murphy, 2006), it can symbolize for covictims that the offender has changed for the better (King, 2003). Offenders often mention the transformative power of religious conversion in their final statements (Smith, 2020), making claims such as, "I am not the same person that I used to be…Christ has changed me" and "I came here a sinner and am leaving a saint" (p. 10) while asking for forgiveness.

Capital punishment does not make much space for remorseful offenders. They have already been deemed to be unremorseful and unredeemable by the court system, and public opinion of them is often influenced by the exaggerated stereotypes of psychopathic serial killers portrayed in the media. And yet, despite the challenges of finding opportunities in the judicial process to express their remorse, there is evidence that some offenders are capable of feeling genuinely sorry for their actions. Even if the number who are remorseful is small, there is value in examining what this remorse might look like, and how it might be received by others.

References

Alesina, A., & La Ferrara, E. (2014). A test of racial bias in capital sentencing. *American Economic Review*, *104*(11), 3397–3433. https://doi.org/10.1257/aer.104.11.3397

Amnesty International (2022). *Amnesty International report 2021/2022. The state of the world's human rights.* www.amnesty.org/en/documents/pol10/4870/2022/en/

Amnesty International (2023). *Death penalty 2022 executions skyrocket.* www.amnesty.org/en/latest/news/2023/05/death-penalty-2022-executions-skyrocket/#tab-global-facts

Baglole, J. S., Tsang, S., Hare, R. D., & Forth, A. E. (2022). Psychopathic expression from early to late adulthood: An item response theory analysis of the Hare Psychopathy Checklist–Revised. *Assessment*, *29*(3), 535–555. https://doi.org/10.1177/1073191120980063

Bandes, S. A. (2014). Remorse, demeanor, and the consequences of mis-interpretation: The limits of law as a window into the soul. *Journal of Law, Religion and State*, *3*(2), 170–199. https://doi.org/10.1163/22124 810-00302004

Bandes, S. A. (2016). Remorse and criminal justice. *Emotion Review*, *8*(1), 14–19. https://doi.org/10.1177/1754073915601222

Banner, S. (2002). *The death penalty*. Harvard University Press.

Barrile, L. G. (2015). I forgive you, but you must die: Murder victim family members, the death penalty, and restorative justice. *Victims & Offenders*, *10*(3), 239–269. https://doi.org/10.1080/15564886.2014.925022

Blume, J. H., Johnson, S. L., Marcus, P., & Paavola, E. (2014). A tale of two (and possibly three) Atkins: Intellectual disability and capital punishment twelve years after the Supreme Court's creation of a cat-egorical bar. *William and Mary Bill of Rights Journal*, *23*(2), 393–414.

Bowers, W. J. (1995). The Capital Jury Project: Rationale, design, and pre-view of early findings. *Indiana Law Journal*, *70*, 1043–1102.

Bowers, W. J., & Pierce, G. L. (1980). Deterrence or brutalization: What is the effect of executions? *Crime & Delinquency*, *26*(4), 453–484. https://doi.org/10.1177/001112878002600402

Bowers, W. J., Steiner, B. D., & Sandys, M. (2001). Death sentencing in black and white: An empirical analysis of the role of jurors' race and jury racial composition. *Journal of Constitutional Law*, *3*(1), 171–274.

Bright, S. B. (2014). The role of race, poverty, intellectual disability, and mental illness in the decline of the death penalty. *University of Richmond Law Review*, *49*, 671–692.

Burton, A. L., Cullen, F. T., Burton Jr, V. S., Graham, A., Butler, L. C., & Thielo, A. J. (2020). Belief in redeemability and punitive public opinion: "Once a criminal, always a criminal" revisited. *Criminal Justice and Behavior*, *47*(6), 712–732. https://doi.org/10.1177/00938 54820913585

Carl, A. E. (2020). Dead wrong: Capital punishment, wrongful convictions, and serious mental illness. *Wrongful Conviction Law Review*, *1*(3), 336–363. https://doi.org/10.29173/wclawr16

Cheng, J. (2010). Frontloading mitigation: The "legal" and the "human" in death penalty defense. *Law & Social Inquiry*, *35*(1), 39–65. https://doi.org/10.1111/j.1747-4469.2009.01177.x

China Justice Observer (2020, November 23). How many crimes are punishable by death in China? China law in one minute. *China Justice Observer*, www.chinajusticeobserver.com/a/how-many-crimes-are-pun ishable-by-death-in-china

Cleckley H. 1941. *The mask of sanity*. Mosby.

Costanzo, M., & Costanzo, S. (1992). Jury decision making in the capital penalty phase: Legal assumptions, empirical findings, and a research agenda. *Law and Human Behavior*, *16*(2), 185–201. https://doi.org/10.1007/BF01044797

Davis, E., & Snell, T. L. (2018). *Capital punishment, 2016* (Report NCJ 251430). U.S. Department of Justice, Bureau of Justice Statistics.

Death Penalty Information Centre (2023a). *Execution database*. https://deathpenaltyinfo.org/database/executions

Death Penalty Information Centre (2023b). *The death penalty in 2022: Year-end report*. https://deathpenaltyinfo.org/facts-and-research/dpic-reports/dpic-year-end-reports/the-death-penalty-in-2022-year-end-report

Death Penalty Information Centre (2023c). *Policy issues: Innocence*. https://deathpenaltyinfo.org/policy-issues/innocence

DeLisi, M., Peters, D. J., Hochstetler, A., Butler, H. D., & Vaughn, M. G. (2023). Psychopathy among condemned capital murderers. *Journal of Forensic Sciences*, *68*(2), 558–567. https://doi.org/10.1111/1556-4029.15188

Dickens, C. (1849, November 13). Mr. Charles Dickens and the execution of the Mannings (letter to the editor). *The Times*. www.charlesdickenspage.com/public-execution.html

ECDHR (2023). *Shedding blood on the issue: Saudi Arabia's unflinching approach to the death penalty*. European Centre for Democracy and Human Rights, www.ecdhr.org/?p=1571

Edens, J. F., Colwell, L. H., Desforges, D. M., & Fernandez, K. (2005). The impact of mental health evidence on support for capital punishment: Are defendants labeled psychopathic considered more deserving of death? *Behavioral Sciences & the Law*, *23*(5), 603–625. https://doi.org/10.1002/bsl.660

Edens, J. F., Davis, K. M., Fernandez Smith, K., & Guy, L. S. (2013). No sympathy for the devil: Attributing psychopathic traits to capital murderers also predicts support for executing them. *Personality Disorders: Theory, Research, and Treatment*, *4*(2), 175–181. https://doi.org/10.1037/a0026442

Eisenberg, T., Garvey, S. P., & Wells, M. T. (1998). But was he sorry? The role of remorse in capital sentencing. *Cornell Law Review, 83*, 1599–1637.

Espy, M. W., & Smykla, J. O. (2016). *Executions in the United States, 1608–2002: The Espy File*. Inter-university Consortium for Political and Social Research. https://doi.org/10.3886/ICPSR08451.v5

Everett, R. S., & Nienstedt, B. C. (1999). Race, remorse, and sentence reduction: Is saying you're sorry enough? *Justice Quarterly*, *16*, 99–122. https://doi.org/10.1080/07418829900094071

Fox, B., & DeLisi, M. (2019). Psychopathic killers: A meta-analytic review of the psychopathy-homicide nexus. *Aggression and Violent Behavior*, *44*, 67–79. https://doi.org/10.1016/j.avb.2018.11.005

Gallop (2023). *In depth: Topics A to Z. The death penalty.* Gallop. https://news.gallup.com/poll/1606/death-penalty.aspx

Garland, D. (2001). *The culture of control: Crime and social order in contemporary society.* University of Chicago Press.

Gross, S. R., O'Brien, B., Hu, C., & Kennedy, E. H. (2014). Rate of false conviction of criminal defendants who are sentenced to death. *Proceedings of the National Academy of Sciences, 111*(20), 7230–7235. https://doi.org/10.1073/pnas.1306417111

Guthke, K. S. (1992). *Last words: variations on a theme in cultural history.* Princeton University Press.

Haney, C. (1995). Social context of capital murder: Social histories and the logic of mitigation. *Santa Clara Law Review, 35*(2), 547–609.

Haney, C., Sontag, L., & Constanzo, S. (1994). Deciding to take a life: Capital juries, sentencing instructions, and the jurisprudence of death. *Journal of Social Issues, 50*, 149–176. https://doi.org/10.1111/j.1540-4560.1994.tb02414.x

Hare, R. D. (1991). *The Hare Psychopathy Checklist–Revised.* Multi-Health Systems.

Hare, R. D. (1996). Psychopathy: A clinical construct whose time has come. *Criminal Justice and Behavior, 23*(1), 25–54. https://doi.org/10.1177/0093854896023001004

Hoag, A. (2020). Valuing black lives: A case for ending the death penalty. *Columbia Human Rights Law Review, 51*, 983–1007.

Hood, R., & Hoyle, C. (2015). *The death penalty: A worldwide perspective.* Oxford University Press.

King, R. (2003). *Don't kill in our names: Families of murder victims speak out against the death penalty.* Rutgers University Press.

Kinnier, R. T., Kernes, J. L., & Dautheribes, T. M. (2000). A short list of universal moral values. *Counseling and Values, 45*(1), 4–16. https:/doi.org/10.1002/j.2161-007X.2000.tb00178.x

Kronenwetter, M. (2001). *Capital punishment: A reference handbook.* 2nd Ed. ABC-CLIO.

LaChance, D. (2007). Last words, last meals, and last stands: Agency and individuality in the modern execution process. *Law & Social Inquiry, 32*(3), 701–724. https://doi.org/10.1111/j.1747-4469.2007.00074.x

Laurence, J. (1960). *A history of capital punishment.* The Citadel Press.

Lombroso-Ferrero, G. (1911). *Criminal man.* GP Putnam's Sons.

Long, W. C. (1999). Karla Faye Tucker: A case for restorative justice. *American Journal of Criminal Law, 27*, 117–127.

Lynch, M., & Haney, C. (2000). Discrimination and instructional comprehension: Guided discretion, racial bias, and the death penalty. *Law and Human Behavior, 24*(3), 337–358. https://doi.org/10.1023/A:1005588221761

Madow, M. (1995). Forbidden spectacle: Executions, the public and the press in nineteenth century New York. *Buffalo Law Review, 43*(2), 461–562.

Maruna, S., & King, A. (2009). Once a criminal, always a criminal? 'Redeemability' and the psychology of punitive public attitudes. *European Journal on Criminal Policy and Research, 15*, 7–24. https://doi.org/10.1007/s10610-008-9088-1

Miley, L. N., Heiss-Moses, E., Cochran, J. K., Heide, K. M., Fogel, S. J., Smith, M. D., & Bejerregaard, B. J. (2020). An examination of the effects of mental disorders as mitigating factors on capital sentencing outcomes. *Behavioral Sciences & the Law, 38*(4), 381–405. https//doi.org/10.1002/bsl.2477

Mogavero, M. C. (2020). An exploratory examination of intellectual disability and mental illness associated with alleged false confessions. *Behavioral Sciences & the Law, 38*(4), 299–316. https//doi.org/10.1002/bsl.2463

Murakawa, N. (2019). Racial innocence: Law, social science, and the unknowing of racism in the US carceral state. *Annual Review of Law and Social Science, 15*, 473–493. https://doi.org/10.1146/annurev-lawsocsci-101518-042649

Murphy, J. G. (2006). Remorse, apology, and mercy. *Ohio State Journal of Criminal Law, 4*, 423–453.

Murphy, J. G. (2007). Forgiveness, self-respect, and the value of resentment. In E. L. Worthington, Jr. (Ed.), *Handbook of forgiveness* (pp. 57–64). Routledge.

Pew Research Centre (2021, June 2). Most Americans favor the death penalty despite concerns about its administration. *Pewresearch.org*. www.pewresearch.org/politics/2021/06/02/most-americans-favor-the-death-penalty-despite-concerns-about-its-administration/

Phillips, S., & Marceau, J. (2020). Whom the state kills. *Harvard Civil Rights-Civil Liberties Law Review, 55*, 585–656. http://dx.doi.org/10.2139/ssrn.3440828

Pyun, J. (2015). When neurogenetics hurts: Examining the use of neuroscience and genetic evidence in sentencing decisions through implicit bias. *California Law Review, 103*(4), 1019–1045.

Randa, L. E. (1997). *Society's final solution: A history and discussion of the death penalty.* University Press of America.

Ross, M. B. (2007). It's time for me to die: An inside look at death row. In M. Mulvey-Roberts, (Ed.), *Writing for their lives: Death row USA* (pp. 91–103). University of Illinois Press.

Ruscio, A. M., Brown, T. A., Chiu, W. T., Sareen, J., Stein, M. B., & Kessler, R. C. (2008). Social fears and social phobia in the USA: Results from the National Comorbidity Survey Replication. *Psychological Medicine, 38*(1), 15–28. https//doi.org/10.1017/S0033291707001699

Sigler, M. (2006). Mercy, clemency, and the case of Karla Faye Tucker. *Ohio State Journal of Criminal Law, 4*, 455–486.

Smith, R. A. (2020). Race, ethnicity, and the functional use of religion when faced with imminent death. *Religions, 11*(10), 77–95. https//doi.org/10.3390/rel11100500

Snell, T. L. (2021). *Capital punishment, 2020.* (Report NCJ 300381). U.S. Department of Justice, Bureau of Justice Statistics.

Steiker, C. S., & Steiker, J. M. (2020). The rise, fall, and afterlife of the death penalty in the United States. *Annual Review of Criminology, 3*, 299–315. https://doi.org/10.1146/annurev-criminol-011518-024721

Stein, R. A. (2017). The history and future of capital punishment in the United States. *San Diego Law Review, 54*, 1–20.

Sundby, S. E. (1998). Capital jury and absolution: The intersection of trial strategy remorse and the death penalty. *Cornell Law Review, 83*(6), 1557–1598.

Texas Department of Criminal Justice (2023). Death row information. www.tdcj.texas.gov/death_row/dr_facts.html

Umbreit, M. S., & Vos, B. (2000). Homicide survivors meet the offender prior to execution: Restorative justice through dialogue. *Homicide Studies, 4*(1), 63–87. https://doi.org/10.1177/1088767900004001004

Vandiver, M., Giacopassi, D. J., & Gathje, P. R. (2002). "I hope someone murders your mother!" An exploration of extreme support for the death penalty. *Deviant Behavior, 23*(4), 385–415. https://doi.org/10.1080/01639620290086440

Vasiljevic, M., & Viki, G. T. (2013). Dehumanization, moral disengagement, and public attitudes to crime and punishment. In P. G. Bain, J. Vaes, & J-P Leyens (Eds.), *Humanness and dehumanization* (pp. 137–154). Psychology Press.

Washington Post (2001, May 3) Post-ABC poll: The death penalty. *Washingtonpost.com.* www.washingtonpost.com/wp-srv/nation/sidebars/polls/050301deathpoll.htm?itid=lk_inline_manual_10

Weisman, R. (2014). *Showing remorse: Law and the social control of emotion.* Routledge.

3   The remorseful offender?

Evidence from their last statements

> I wish to apologize to the people who I have hurt and I ask
> for their forgiveness. I don't deserve it, but I do ask for it.
>
> (Jack Trawick, executed in Alabama in 2009;
> Clark County Prosecuting Attorney, 2009)

In 2009, immediately before he was executed, Jack Trawick made the above statement to the people gathered to witness his death. While Trawick could have spent his final moments denying his guilt, seeking a reprieve or pardon, or angrily speaking out about the injustice of the death penalty, he instead chose to apologize for his crime.

The final words of executed inmates are unique for many reasons. First, unlike most people, they are fully aware of their pending death (down to the exact date and time) and have time to think about what they will say in their final words. Although people who have a terminal illness are aware that they might die soon, they do not know precisely when it will happen, and they may not be in good enough health to say what they would like to say when the time comes. Second, individuals on death row know that last words are expected of them and that they will have an audience. Some decline to say anything, but most say something. Third, the people who will be present for an inmate's last words can include both friends and potential foes: Their family may attend but so might their victims' family members. Typically when people die they are not in the presence of people who might have very mixed feelings about them and might be there specifically because

DOI: 10.4324/9781003384946-3

they want to watch them die. When deciding what to say, inmates might struggle with how to balance their message of love for their family and message of remorse for those who are only there to watch them be executed.

This chapter takes an in-depth look at these final words and considers what they can tell us about offenders on death row and remorse. Using their statements as a dataset, it explores both the themes of their statements and the actual words they used, in order to determine whether (and how) they might show evidence of remorse.

The last statement

What can these final words tell us about the internal emotional state of inmates immediately before they are executed? One line of reasoning suggests that because they have nothing left to lose they have no reason to lie. In law, the final words of dying individuals are called "dying declarations." Historically these dying declarations were considered to be sincere and trustworthy because it was believed that no one would want to face God immediately after having lied. In fact, the legal maxim *Nemo moriturus praesumitur mentire* is interpreted to mean that a dying person should be presumed to be telling the truth. It is sometimes translated as, "a man would not meet his maker with a lie on his lips" (Creo, 2016, p. 70). One flaw in this reasoning is that it is based on the Christian belief that there is an afterlife – that we meet God when we die and are judged on our suitability for Heaven. Christians might believe that lying right before death might affect their chances of a good afterlife, but people from other religions, or non-religious people, might not. For them, an untruthful dying declaration might post no existential issues at all.

A different line of reasoning suggests that the last words of criminals cannot be trusted. In 1720, a book detailing the last words of executed state prisoners from the previous 300 years cautioned that "it must be admitted than an account of his preceding life…must certainly contribute something toward forming a right judgment of him" (Anonymous, 1720, p. A2). More recently, it has been argued that while spontaneous last words might capture the sincere feelings of someone who did not have advanced warning about their pending death, having too much time to think about one's last words makes them more prone to self-serving fabrications (Orenstein, 2010).

Last statements as "data"

Since capital punishment was reinstated in the United States in 1976, the Texas Department of Justice has been documenting the last statements of the inmates it has executed. These last statements, posted on the Texas Department of Justice website, are an interesting and convenient dataset. It may seem odd to refer to them as a "dataset," because we often think of a dataset as a spreadsheet full of numbers. However, almost anything can be considered a dataset if it can be analysed in order to extract meaning from it. Data that is in numerical form is referred to as quantitative data, and data that is in text, visual, or some other non-numerical form is considered qualitative data. These hundreds of last statements, when considered as a group, make up an impressive qualitative dataset that could potentially help us to understand both the motivations of convicted offenders and, more generally, human reactions to mortality.

A number of researchers have attempted to do just this over the past 20 or so years. The most common method they have used is content analysis, which involves analysing the statements to find common themes. These content analyses tend to be either strictly qualitative (i.e., non-numerical), where the researchers identify the general themes used in the last statements, or they are a combination of qualitative and quantitative techniques, where the researchers identify the main themes and estimate the number of statements containing each theme. Both methods are valid and effective ways to summarize the data, helping to clarify what kinds of things inmates include in their final statements and revealing what the most common themes are.

General themes in last statements

Just as the population of people on death row is diverse, so are the things they say in their final statements. Some are angry, some are loving, and some are both. Some claim innocence, and some take full responsibility for their crimes. And some chose to say nothing at all. While there isn't really a "typical" last statement, there are some commonalities and themes.

The first academic article analysing themes in last statements was published in 2005. It described a qualitative content analysis of the last statements of the 237 individuals who had been executed between 1997 and 2005 (Heflick, 2005). Heflick (2005) identified six themes: afterlife belief, silence, claims of innocence, activism, love/ appreciation, and forgiveness. Since this initial work, there have been many other thematic analyses of death row statements. While the labelling of the themes might change, there is a fair amount of consistency in the broad classification of what is mentioned in these last statements. In addition to the themes mentioned above, researchers have also identified themes of spirituality/religion (Cooney & Phillips, 2013; Foley & Kelly, 2018; Smith, 2020; Upton et al., 2017; Vollum & Longmire, 2009), gratitude (Upton et al., 2017; Vollum & Longmire, 2009), apology and remorse (Cooney & Phillips, 2013; Eaton, 2014; Eaton & Theuer, 2009; Rice et al., 2009), and self-presentation (Schuck & Ward, 2008).

What is perhaps most remarkable about these themes is that they are more positive than negative. Religion, forgiveness, and love appear frequently, along with accountability and peace/ acceptance. While injustice/anger (Rice et al., 2009; Vollum & Longmire, 2009) and claims of innocence do factor into some of the statements, positive themes clearly outweigh negative themes. This finding has been confirmed in research using linguistic analysis, which uses software to quantify the actual words themselves, classifying them as either positive or negative in tone. Overall, the statements have been found to contain more words that are positive in tone (such as love, joy, happy) than words that are negative in tone (such as hate, sad, angry) (Goranson et al., 2017; Hirschmüller & Egloff, 2016). In an effort to demonstrate that the last statements contained more positive language than would be expected, Goranson and colleagues (2017) asked a sample of people who were not in prison to imagine what they might say if they were about to be executed. Surprisingly, these imagined last statements were less positive than the last statements of the people who actually were about to be executed.

Rather than using this – their final chance to connect with others – as an act of defiance or a last-ditch effort to change their fate, many of these offenders instead choose messages of positivity and love. The reason for this is unclear: Perhaps people really do become more positive when they are about to die (Goranson et al.,

2017; Kashdan et al., 2014), or perhaps this positivity is a defence mechanism against the existential threat of death (Hirschmüller & Egloff, 2016; Schuck & Ward, 2008). What is clear, however, is that this heightened positivity does not fit with the common perception of inmates on death row as monsters who are incapable of emotion, love, or empathy.

We'll return to this point later; for now, at the very least, what this research reveals is that the last statements are valuable as a dataset and that this topic is worthy of more study. Although death row offenders have received a certain amount of attention by researchers and the media, very little of what is written about them comes from their own words. While some grant interviews while on death row, many do not. In addition, they generally do not speak to the media the day they are executed. Given the lack of any other available data on this population at the particular point in time in which they are facing their death, the uniqueness and potential value of these narratives is unquestionable. They can provide insight into the minds of the individuals who made them and also, perhaps, into basic human responses to the idea of death and mortality.

Remorse in last statements

Many of the studies that have examined general themes in last statements have identified some form of remorse as a theme, whether it is framed as seeking forgiveness (e.g., Heflick, 2005), making an apology (e.g., Eaton & Theuer, 2009; Foley & Kelly, 2018), or repenting (Rice et al., 2009). Because the identification and coding of remorse might differ between studies it is difficult to quantify exactly how many offenders express remorse, but generally these studies have found that about one-third of offenders apologize or otherwise express some form of repentance or remorse (Cooney & Phillips, 2013; Eaton & Theuer, 2009, Rice et al. 2009). Identifying remorse in these statements is not difficult – the last statement by Jack Trawick at the beginning of this chapter is a good example of a clear apology ("I want to apologize…") and asking for forgiveness ("I ask for their forgiveness. I don't deserve it, but I do ask for it.").

Some studies have looked specifically at indicators of remorse in the last statements in an effort to understand which inmates apologize, and why. The main findings from these studies indicate that there is not one specific "type" of offender who is more likely to apologize – demographic variables such as age, race, and level of education do not make inmates more or less likely to apologize in their last statement (Eaton & Theuer, 2009). There is some evidence of regional differences in apologies, however. Eaton (2014), using last statements from across the United States, compared the apologies of inmates executed in southern states and non-southern states and found that inmates executed in southern states were more likely to apologize in their last statement, although there was no evidence that these apologies were any more genuine or sincere than apologies from the non-southern states. It may be that these southern apologies are the result of southern politeness norms, whereby inmates will say "I'm sorry" because they are following a cultural script and not necessarily because they feel truly remorseful. Rice and colleagues (2009) found evidence of an external variable not related to the inmate that can predict whether an inmate will apologize. They explored whether the presence of the victims' family members had any effect on whether inmates expressed remorse in their final statements. Using 1996, when Texas began allowing covictims to attend executions, as the dividing line, they found that inmates were more likely to show repentance after 1996 than before. Although there could be other factors that made apologies more likely after 1996, this research suggests that inmates are more likely to express their remorse if the family members of their victims are present.

Other research has examined other factors within the last statement that tend to appear along with apologies and remorse. Cooney and Phillips (2013) found that those individuals who mentioned God in their last statement were more likely to make an apology, and the more mentions of God that were made, the higher the chance of an apology. Eaton and Theuer (2009) found that other remorse-related variables tended to go along with apologies. Inmates who apologized in their last statement also tended to take responsibility for their actions, ask for forgiveness, and show empathy and sincerity. Foley and Kelly (2018) found across two studies that inmates who apologized also tended to say things that indicated that they felt that the execution would resolve the intense pain and trauma they were feeling, referred to by the researchers as "unbearable psychological pain" (p. 400).

The research study

Overview

With the exception of the research comparing apologies from southern and non-southern inmates (Eaton, 2014), the research specifically focusing on remorse in last statements uses only the last statements of inmates executed in Texas. There is good reason for this: Texas is the only state that makes the last statements of its inmates publicly available, and it is a large sample to work with. As of Summer 2023, a total of 1571 individuals have been executed in the United States since capital punishment was reinstated in 1976, and 583 of them (approximately one-third) were in Texas (Death Penalty Information Center, 2023). Because the execution process in Texas includes steps for recording, documenting, and releasing the last statements, there is consistency in the collection of this data (although it may still be subject to bias, omissions, or transcription issues). It also means that the research on last statements mostly draws from the same dataset, which allows for easier comparisons between the individual studies.

The limitation of focusing only on executed inmates in Texas is that the findings may not be generalizable to the rest of the country. The United States is a large, diverse country, and although there is federal oversight, the individual states have a fair amount of autonomy over their own laws and processes. This has resulted in differences between the states in, for example, gun laws, social services, education, immigration policies, and unemployment rates, all of which could affect who commits a crime and how they are treated once they are in the justice system. Texas is unique in many ways, from its size and geography (Meinig, 2010) to its cultural history, and individuals sentenced to death in Texas may be different in some ways from those sentenced to death in other states that still have capital punishment. While Texas accounts for one-third of the US executions, the literature has largely ignored the remaining two-thirds of executed inmates.

Our understanding of remorse in the last statements of executed inmates is incomplete in part because of the focus on Texas but also because the existing research is not up to date. There is no single study that includes all of the last statements from the time the death penalty was re-introduced in 1976 to the present. The remainder of this chapter addresses both of these gaps in the data by presenting a comprehensive analysis of remorse in the last statements of all individuals executed in the United States between 1976 and 2022.

The data

Executions by state

The dataset for this analysis contains information about all of the executions in the United States since the death penalty was

Table 3.1 Executions by State (1976–2022)

State	Total executions	Percentage of total
Texas	582	37.4
Oklahoma	118	7.6
Virginia	114	7.3
Florida	98	6.3
Missouri	96	6.2
Georgia	76	4.9
Alabama	70	4.5
Ohio	57	3.7
North Carolina	43	2.8
South Carolina	43	2.8
Arizona	37	2.4
Arkansas	35	2.2
Louisiana	28	1.8
Mississippi	23	1.5
Indiana	20	1.3
Delaware	16	1.0
California	14	0.9
Tennessee	13	0.8
Illinois	12	0.8
Nevada	12	0.8
Utah	7	0.4
Maryland	6	0.4
South Dakota	5	0.3
Washington	5	0.3
Idaho	3	0.2
Kentucky	3	0.2
Montana	3	0.2
Nebraska	3	0.2
Pennsylvania	3	0.2
Oregon	2	0.1

Note: States not shown had 1 or no executions.

reinstated in 1976, up until the end of 2022 (a total of 1558). Table 3.1 is a breakdown of how many executions have been carried out in each state in this time period, listed in order of magnitude. The table clearly shows that executions are not evenly balanced between the states. Texas, with 582, accounts for more than one-third of all executions in the United States. Oklahoma, Virginia, Florida, Missouri, Georgia, and Alabama combined make up another one-third of the total executions, and the remaining one-third is comprised of all the other states.

Inmate characteristics

The names of executed inmates and basic information about their age, gender, and race and the number and gender of the victims were taken from the Death Penalty Information Center (2023), which maintains an up-to-date list of all executions. Table 3.2 summarizes this demographic information. Almost all of the executed inmates were male, and just over half were White, one-third were Black, and the rest were Hispanic or Asian, with only a few not fitting into any of these categories. They ranged in age from 22 to 83 at the time of their execution, with an average age of about 42 years. Their victims were fairly evenly split between male and female, although in almost 13% of the cases no information about the victims could be found.

The last statements

The last statements from Texas executions were collected from the Texas Department of Criminal Justice (2023) website. The last statements from the rest of the United States were more challenging to find, since there is no general repository for them. A number of steps were taken to locate them. Many of the last statements were found on the website of the Prosecuting Attorney of Clark County, Indiana (2023). This website provides information about executions from 1976 to 2014, including the last statements, where available. Internet search strategies for the remaining executions (those conducted after 2014 and any last statements that could not be found on Clark Prosecutor website) included a general search for the inmate's name and news articles published within a week following the execution. Despite these efforts, the exact text of the

Table 3.2 Characteristics of executed inmates

Offender characteristic	Total (percentage of total)
Sex of inmate	
Male	1541 (98.9%)
Female	17 (1.1%)
Race of inmate	
White	877 (56.3%)
Black	526 (33.8%)
Hispanic	132 (8.5%)
Asian	6 (0.4%)
Other	17 (1.1%)
Age of inmate at time of execution	
Average (with standard deviation)	42.24 years ($SD = 9.94$)
Range	22 – 83
Length of time on death row	
Average (with standard deviation)	13.51 years ($SD = 6.54$)
Range	<1 – 40
Sex of victim(s) [a]	
Male	570 (36.6%)
Female	558 (35.8%)
Both	231 (14.8%)
Unknown	199 (12.8%)

Note:
[a] This represents the number of cases rather than the number of actual victims. "Both" represents a case where there were multiple victims with a mixture of males and females.

last statements of many of the non-Texas inmates could not be found. In some cases the exact wording was not available but a news article described elements of the last statement. Table 3.3 shows the breakdown of how many inmates made a last statement.

Findings

Content analysis

This analysis focused mainly on variables related to remorse, so the content analysis was restricted to specific terms and themes. In order to compare the findings of this new expanded dataset to our earlier findings (Eaton & Theuer, 2009), the same variables

Table 3.3 Inmates who made a last statement

	Total	Texas	Non-Texas
Inmate made a last statement	1102 (70.7%)	462 (79%)	640 (66%)
Inmate did not make a last statement	368 (23.6%)	75 (13%)	293 (30%)
Unknown	88 (5.6%)	45 (8%)	43 (4%)
Total	1558	582	976

and terminology were used (described below). The coding involved reading each last statement in its entirety, but without any additional information such as the nature of the crime, details about the offender or the victims, or the location. Each of the variables were coded as either being present (coded as "1") or absent (coded as "0") in each last statement. A subset of these codes were verified by a second coder. In our first research study using this dataset, two researchers read and coded the entire set of statements, and the inter-rater reliability (Cohen's kappa) was very high. Cohen's kappa ranges from 0 to 1.0, where 0 would mean that there was no agreement between the two coders and 1.0 would mean perfect agreement between the coders. In our prior study, Cohen's kappa was above .89 for every variable, and most variables had a Cohen's kappa higher than .94 (Eaton & Theuer, 2009). This suggests that coding for specific remorse-related variables in these statements is a fairly objective task – there is little disagreement over whether the variables are present or not. Therefore, for this expanded dataset, codes were validated for a subset of the statements, with very high agreement.

This analysis included the remorse-related variables identified in prior research, including sentiments directly related to remorse, such as whether the inmate apologized, took responsibility for the crime, and asked for forgiveness, and also variables that might be seen as indicators of remorse, such as whether they showed empathy, remorse, and sincerity. Table 3.4 shows the number of last statements containing each variable.

Apology. The most common remorse-related sentiment in the last statements was an apology. A total of 30% of inmates offered an apology in their final statement. They were considered to have

Table 3.4 Frequency of coded variables

Variable	Total
Apologized	331 (30%)
Took responsibility	137 (12.4%)
Asked for forgiveness	147 (13.3%)
Showed empathy	172 (15.6%)
Showed remorse	87 (7.9%)
Showed sincerity	294 (26.7%)
Mentioned religion	435 (39.4%)
Claimed innocence	146 (13.2%)

apologized if they said they were sorry or that they wanted to apologize. For some, their last statement was brief and only included the words "I'm sorry." For others, the apology was included in a longer statement about why they were sorry:

> First of all, I would like to give my sincere apology to [the victim's] family. We caused a lot of heartache, grief, pain, and suffering, and I am sorry.
>
> (Michael Hall, executed in Texas in 2011;
> Texas Department of Criminal Justice, 2011)

Responsibility. Recall from Chapter 1 that apologies tend to be more effective when the person who caused the harm takes responsibility for their actions. A full apology includes explaining what you are sorry for. In the last statements, inmates were considered to have accepted responsibility if they specifically said they were responsible for the crime or if they described what they had done. Not all who apologized did this: A total of 12.4% of inmates took responsibility for their crime in their final statement. Often, but not always, taking responsibility was accompanied by an admission of guilt:

> I am guilty for what I'm here for, and I take full responsibility for my actions. And to [the victim's] family, I say I'm sorry that I can't undo it. And I'm sorry to my family for all the pain I've caused.
>
> (Kenneth Hogan, executed in Oklahoma in 2014;
> Clark County Prosecuting Attorney, 2014a)

Forgiveness. A less direct way of apologizing is to ask for forgiveness. A total of 13.3% of inmates asked for forgiveness in their final statement. Sometimes they directly asked for forgiveness:

> I want to ask for forgiveness...I'm sorry for everything I brought upon her. I'm sorry for the pain, sorrow I brought on her and her family and kids. I'm sorry to all of you for the same thing. I guess I'm going to go now. Bye y'all.
>
> (Larry Jackson, executed in Oklahoma in 2003;
> Clark County Prosecuting Attorney, 2003)

Sometimes they expressed a hope that the family members of their victims could eventually forgive them:

> I hope that you could forgive me, but if you don't I understand. I don't think I could forgive anyone who would have killed my children.
>
> (James Bigby, executed in Texas in 2017;
> Texas Department of Criminal Justice, 2017)

Sometimes their requests for forgiveness were directed towards the family members of their victims, sometimes towards their own family, sometimes both, and sometimes God.

Empathy. Although it is not directly related to remorse, the degree of empathy the inmates expressed in their last statements is an indicator of how authentic and genuine their words were. Empathy was coded as an understanding of how the victim's family felt at the loss of their loved one or an understanding of how the victim might have felt during the crime. A total of 15.6% of inmates expressed empathy in their final statement. Sometimes empathy was expressed as an acknowledgement that the pain of the loss of the victim's loved one was ongoing, and that perhaps the execution could bring them some relief:

> I hope this brings you comfort and eases your pain some.
>
> (Abdullah Hameen, executed in Delaware in 2001;
> Clark County Prosecuting Attorney, 2001)

Remorse. Sometimes inmates specifically mentioned that they felt remorse for the crime, or expressed regret or bad feelings about their actions. It is difficult to determine if this indicates actual remorse – the inmate might not understand what true remorse is, or they may be simply equating it with saying they are sorry – but this was considered to be different from simply saying "I'm sorry." A total of 7.9% of inmates expressed remorse in their final statement. This example was coded as remorse because the inmate not only said they were remorseful but they also expressed regret and tried to atone for the crime:

> I would like to express to the [victim's] family and anyone else I hurt how deeply remorseful I am for everything I did. I know these are mere words and cannot erase the damage I did. For the last 20 years, I've tried to do one good deed every single day to replace the loss my actions took from this world. If nothing, I hope you get peace and closure.
>
> (Thomas Loden, executed in Mississippi in 2022; Warren & Jackson, 2022)

Sincerity. The degree of sincerity in their last statement is another indicator of how authentic or genuine they were. If the inmate expressed love or gratitude towards the victim's family, or if they appeared to be earnest in their statements, they were coded as being sincere. A total of 26.7% of inmates appeared to be sincere in their final statement. This statement was coded as being sincere because the inmate appeared to show genuine concern for the victims' families:

> There are no words to describe the pain and suffering that you have gone through all these years. That is something that I cannot take back from you all…I am sorry that is has taken 14 years to get closure. If it would have brought closure or brought her back, I would have done this years ago, I promise, I promise. My family all knows the sincerity in my heart when I say these words to you.
>
> (Timothy Titsworth, executed in Texas in 2006; Texas Department of Criminal Justice, 2006)

This category was somewhat challenging to code because sincerity is more subjective than some of the other variables – inmates rarely said specifically that they were sincere; it was more often implied in what they said. It was more straightforward to identify a lack of sincerity. This well-known last statement would not have been coded as sincere:

> Okay I've been hanging around this popsicle stand way too long. Before I leave, I want to tell you all. When I die, bury me deep, lay two speakers at my feet, put some headphones on my head and rock and roll me when I'm dead.
>
> (Douglas Roberts, executed in Texas in 2005;
> Texas Department of Criminal Justice, 2005)

Religion/Spirituality. A total of 39.4% of inmates mentioned religion, God, Allah, or spirituality in their final statement. There were many different uses of religion in the statements. Many mentioned how their faith helped them prepare for the execution:

> My trials and transgressions have been many. But thanks be to my Lord and savior, Jesus Christ, I have a new home in his heavenly kingdom.
>
> (William Rousan, executed in Missouri in 2014;
> Clark County Prosecuting Attorney, 2014b)

Some expressed the hope that faith would allow the victim's family members to find peace, or as reassurance that they would see their loved one again:

> I'm sorry, I'm sorry. God will let you see her again. Freddy, I love you, I kept my promise. Thank you for being here for me.
>
> (Donald Beaty, executed in Arizona in 2011;
> Clark County Prosecuting Attorney, 2011)

Others did not address their own family or the victim's family, and chose to only say a prayer or quote from a religious text:

> There's no god but God, and Mohammed is his prophet.
>
> (Vernon Smith, executed in Ohio in 2010;
> Clark County Prosecuting Attorney, 2010)

Innocence. Innocence, while not an indicator of remorse, can help explain why, in some instances, an inmate might not apologize or show remorse. A total of 13.2% of inmates used their final statement to claim innocence. At times their words were accompanied by anger:

> I am innocent, innocent, innocent. Make no mistake about this; I owe society nothing.
>
> (Leonel Herrera, executed in Texas in 1993; Texas Department of Criminal Justice, 1993)

At times their claims of innocence were more matter-of-fact or rational:

> I want the world to know that I'm innocent and that I've found peace. Let's ride.
>
> (Carl Johnson, executed in Texas in 1995; Texas Department of Criminal Justice, 1995)

Sometimes they continued to try to provide evidence of their innocence right up until the last minute:

> If you look at the transcripts, I didn't kill Mr. Newman and I didn't rob your house. There are two people still alive. I was just there. When I saw you in the truck driving away, I could have killed you but I didn't. I'm not a killer… It wasn't me that harmed and stole all of your stuff. If you look at the transcripts you will see.
>
> (Ricky Lewis, executed in Texas in 2013; Texas Department of Criminal Justice, 2013)

Predictors of apology

The numbers above tell us the frequency of the individual remorse-related variables, but they don't tell us how, or whether, they were used together in their last statements. Making an apology, on its own, does not necessarily indicate that the inmate felt remorseful. A better indicator of remorse might be to assess whether an inmate's apology could be predicted by the presence of variables that prior research has identified as being related to apology. In other words, do those who say they are sorry also take responsibility, show empathy and remorse, and appear to be sincere? One way to determine this is with a logistic regression, which is used to analyse how well a set of variables predicts an outcome, or dependent, variable. By using apology as the outcome variable and the remorse-related variables as predictor variables, we can determine how well the remorse-related variables predict, or are connected to, whether the offender made an apology or not.

Table 3.5 shows the results of the logistic regression. The set of remorse-related variables included taking responsibility, asking for forgiveness, showing empathy, showing remorse, and being sincere. Although religion/spirituality is not directly related to apology, it was included because there is research that suggests that those who are higher in religiosity are more likely to apologize in their last statements (Cooney & Philips, 2013).

The overall model was statistically significant. This means that the group of variables was able to distinguish between who would apologize in their last statement and who would not. In other words, if you knew whether someone took responsibility, showed empathy and remorse, appeared sincere, and mentioned religion, you would be able to accurately predict whether they would also say they were sorry. The statistic for this overall test of the model is the chi-square test: χ^2 (6, $N = 1102$) = 491.04, $p < .001$. The model as a whole explained between 36% (Cox and Snell R square) and 51% (Nagelkerke R square) of the variance in apology, and correctly classified 84.4% of cases.

In examining the individual variables and their ability to correctly predict apology, all of the remorse-related variables except empathy were significant predictors – the "p" column in Table 3.5

Table 3.5 Predictors of apology

Predictor	β	$SE \beta$	Wald's χ^2	df	p	Odds ratio
Responsibility	1.73	.31	31.53	1	<.001	5.66
Asking for forgiveness	1.21	.23	22.78	1	<.001	3.35
Empathy	.41	.28	2.18	1	.14	1.50
Remorse	.72	.33	4.67	1	.03	2.05
Sincere	2.29	.22	106.49	1	<.001	9.84
Religion	.00	.18	.00	1	.999	1.00
Constant	−2.16	.13	263.59	1	<.001	.12

shows that responsibility, asking for forgiveness, remorse, and sincerity were all less than $p = .05$, which indicates statistical significance. The strongest predictor of apology was showing sincerity. The odds ratio for this variable is 9.84, which means that those who showed sincerity were 9.84 times more likely to apologize than those who did not show sincerity. The next strongest predictor of apology was taking responsibility, with an odds ratio of 5.66, followed by asking for forgiveness, with an odds ratio of 3.35, and showing remorse, with an odds ratio of 2.05.

Interestingly, religion did not significantly predict apology. This is not consistent with prior research that has shown a relationship between religion and remorse in the last statements. Because that research focused only on Texas, it could be that the relationship between religion and apology is stronger for Texans than it is for the rest of the country. It could also be a coding issue. In this analysis, the coding included any mention of religion, regardless of how it was used (i.e., in anger or in the spirit of peace). For example, a number of inmates quoted some variation of a Bible verse (Luke 23:34) – "Forgive them for they know not what they do," which was coded as mentioning religion, even if the inmate used it to express frustration with the justice system. Other research might have only coded an inmate as mentioning religion if they mentioned it in a positive or loving way.

Regional differences in apology

The proportion of inmates who made an apology in their final statement did not differ significantly between the states, although there were some minor differences. Table 3.6 shows the 8 states

Table 3.6 State differences in rates of apology

Below average (less than 30%)	Above average (higher than 30%)
Alabama (25.7%)	Georgia (39.6%)
Florida (24.2%)	Ohio (36.7%)
Missouri (21.3%)	Oklahoma (36%)
Virginia (22.9%)	Texas (31.7%)

with more than 50 executions in total. Those falling below the 30% apology rate were Alabama, Florida, Missouri, and Virginia. The states with an apology rate higher than the 30% average were Georgia, Ohio, Oklahoma, and Texas.

Linguistic analysis

The content analysis of the remorse-related themes in the last statements showed that a little less than one-third of inmates offered an apology in their last statement, and that these apologies were moderately connected to other indicators of remorse. It could be said that these findings show the conscious, deliberate attempts of the inmates to deliver a certain message. For instance, if they wanted to offer an apology, there are different ways to say it, but the general idea is to say they were sorry or that they wanted to apologize. Another way to analyse their last statements is to look beyond the themes and focus instead on the actual words used. This can also be a valid and informative way to analyse last statements because an individual might have an idea of the things they *should* say in their last statement, but their choice of words might give additional insight into their underlying feelings.

Previous research analysed the last statements of inmates in Texas for positive and negative language and found significantly more words that were positive than negative in tone (Goranson et al., 2017; Hirschmüller & Egloff, 2016). In an attempt to see if this finding held true for inmates across the United States and not just for those in Texas, we conducted a linguistic analysis of the entire set of statements (Eaton & Roul, 2023). Using Linguistic Analysis and Word Count software (LIWC-22; Pennebaker et al., 2022), we found that the average percentage of positive words in the last statements was 9.74% and the average percentage of negative words was 2.43%. A comparison of the means using a paired-samples t-test showed that the difference between positive and negative words was statistically significant: Inmates used significantly more positive than negative words, $t(1094) = 18.85$, $p < .001$.

We also wanted to know whether these proportions of positive and negative words were typical of the way people talk. The creators of the LIWC-22 software provide base rates of positive and negative language in other forms of speech or writing, such as blogs, novels, news media, speeches, Twitter, and even Yelp. They found that, on average, the percentage of positive language in these forms of writing is 3.49% (Boyd et al., 2022). With an average proportion of positive words of 9.74%, the last statements were more positive, on average, than these other forms of communication. The same was not true for negative language. The base rate calculated by Boyd and colleagues (2022) was 1.54%, which is a bit lower than the 2.43% found in the last statements. Overall, these findings show that the last statements do tend to be more positive than negative, and are, in fact, more positive than one might expect from someone who knows they are about to die.

What last statements tell us about remorse

These findings indicate that 30% of offenders apologized, and slightly less than that appeared to be sincere in their comments directed to the victim's family. Fewer of them took responsibility for their crime, asked for forgiveness, or appeared to show remorse. Given that apologies are more effective if they include these sentiments, what do these findings mean? Clearly some offenders do apologize, but are they actually remorseful? The logistic regression analysis showed that these variables did tend to occur together, in that those who took responsibility, asked for forgiveness, showed remorse, and appeared to be sincere towards the victim's family were more likely to apologize. This can be taken as evidence that at least some of the last statements contained many of the elements of a good apology and might indicate that the inmate was truly remorseful. In addition, the last statements contained more positive-focused than negative-focused language. The fact that many inmates apologized and that the statements overall were surprisingly positive suggests that not all individuals on death row are the cold, unfeeling monsters that they are sometimes assumed to be.

This could be viewed as an overly optimistic way to interpret the findings. An alternative view is that not many inmates were remorseful. Less than one-third of the last statements included an apology, and even fewer included the other elements of remorse. Given how heinous their crimes were, unless they were innocent (as 13% claimed to be), all of them should have been remorseful. Why didn't more of them apologize? One reason is that they were truly sorry but did not know how to adequately express their remorse. Ultimately this is impossible to know, but a strong case could be made for this explanation. Chapter 2 listed a number of reasons why showing remorse on death row might be difficult: the context is rigid and sterile, the inmate might lack the skills or mental ability to make an articulate apology, and their anger at an unfair system might overshadow their remorse. For all of these reasons and more, it might be especially challenging for them to make a full apology in their final statement. Consider the context in which the last statement is offered. The offender is about to be executed and has one final opportunity to speak to both his/her own family members and the victim's family. There may be a time limit on how long he/she may speak. The combination of being faced with one's death and being expected to say something meaningful in front of family members, prison officials, the press, and the victim's family would likely cause an inordinate amount of stress. In addition to these external stressors, offenders may not have the tools to clearly articulate their feelings. It takes courage and a certain amount of inner strength to admit to and take responsibility for one's failings (Exline & Baumeister, 2000), and incarcerated offenders, who often feel powerless, vulnerable, and emotionally empty (Johnson, 1979), may not have the inner resources to do this. In their analysis of a subset of Texas death row statements, Foley and Kelley (2018) identified a variable they called "unbearable psychological pain" (p. 400), which was characterized by sentiments made by the inmate indicating that they felt that death would stop the intolerable pain they were feeling. Those inmates who apologized reported higher unbearable psychological pain, which suggests that apologies were effortful and costly for this group.

According to terror management theory (Greenberg et al., 1986), when we become aware of our own mortality it creates existential anxiety, or terror. When we feel this terror we tend to become self-protective and less able to show weakness or vulnerability. An inmate who is about to be executed would be keenly aware of their mortality, which might make it even harder for them admit to their own moral failings by taking responsibility and apologizing to the loved ones of their victims. Sister Helen Prejean, a well-known opponent of the death penalty, makes this point well when she ponders why Robert Willie, a convicted serial killer on death row in Louisiana, did not express any remorse for his crimes:

> Remorse presupposes enough self-forgetfulness to feel the pain of others. Can Robert Willie do that? I doubt it and wonder whether his death sentence makes his own repentance even more difficult. *Someone is trying to kill him*, and this must rivet his energies on his own survival, not the pain of others [italics in original].
>
> (Prejean, 1994, p. 144)

Taken together, these factors suggest that, rather than asking why more offenders do not apologize or are not making "better" apologies, we should be asking how they manage to apologize at all. Given the stressors present in their final moments, the fact that some of them are able to think about their victims' families at all is remarkable.

The limitations of using last statements as a data source

Although the dataset of last statements is unique, expansive, and accessible, it is important to note that it is also inherently flawed. One challenge with this dataset is that it is very difficult to determine how accurate it is. Executions are not open to the public; nor are recordings of them made available. Thus, it is impossible to verify whether they have been documented accurately – they might include transcription errors, bias on the part of the individual reporting them, and omissions. These challenges are compounded if last statements of inmates from states other than Texas are included in the dataset, because often they are not part of official documents from the institution and are instead taken from media sources. Even in the Texas system, where there is a clear process for documenting the last statements, sometimes non-English phrases within last statements are translated but sometimes they are not, and obscenities are often removed from the text before it is made available. Unlike other types of qualitative data where an original recording exists and the transcription can be checked against it for accuracy, we can only assume that the written documentation of last statements is an accurate reflection of what was actually said.

Another challenge is with interpreting to what extent the words in the last statement actually reflect what the offender feels. Although there is much we can learn from a written text, it is missing the non-verbal cues, such as tone of voice, body language, and facial expressions that can help us understand what the offender's underlying emotions were. The last statements do not include, for example, information about whether the offender was crying or not, whether they spoke loudly or quietly, or even whether they appeared to show sadness or remorse. Recall from Chapter 1 that embodied remorse – the non-verbal cues that offenders display in the courtroom – is sometimes given more weight that the actual words the offender says. Without this, we can only infer the offender's emotional state from the words that they use in their last statement.

Another challenge is with the generalizability of the statements. Because not every offender provides a last statement – they are allowed to decline to say anything – there is a limit to how much we can assume that our findings and conclusions about the last statements accurately represent the thoughts and feelings of those who did not make a last statement. It is possible that those inmates who decline to make a last statement are different in some important ways from those who do. Maybe they are less likely to be remorseful, or maybe they were actually more likely to feel remorse. Maybe some of them had already apologized either at their trial or some point during their incarceration and did not feel the need to do it again in their final statement. There is no way to know whether those who declined to speak at their execution were remorseful or not, and since we only had final statements from 71% of the inmates, we cannot assume that our findings accurately represent that other 29%.

References

Anonymous. (1720). *The dying speeches and behaviour of the several state prisoners that have been executed the last 300 years. Being a proper supplement to the state-tryals.* Brotherton & Meadows.

Boyd, R. L., Ashokkumar, A., Seraj, S., & Pennebaker, J. W. (2022). *The development and psychometric properties of LIWC-22.* University of Texas at Austin. www.liwc.app

Clark County Prosecuting Attorney (2001). Abdullah Tanzil Hameen. *ClarkProsecutor.org.* www.clarkprosecutor.org/html/death/US/hameen715.htm

Clark County Prosecuting Attorney (2003). Larry Kenneth Jackson. *ClarkProsecutor.org*. www.clarkprosecutor.org/html/death/US/jackson 846.htm

Clark County Prosecuting Attorney (2009). Jack Harrison Trawick. *ClarkProsecutor.org*. www.clarkprosecutor.org/html/death/US/traw ick1168.htm

Clark County Prosecuting Attorney (2010). Vernon Lamont Smith. *ClarkProsecutor.org*. www.clarkprosecutor.org/html/death/US/smith1 189.htm

Clark County Prosecuting Attorney (2011). Donald Edward Beaty. *ClarkProsecutor.org*. www.clarkprosecutor.org/html/death/US/beaty1 253.htm

Clark County Prosecuting Attorney (2014a). Kenneth Eugene Hogan. *ClarkProsecutor.org*. www.clarkprosecutor.org/html/death/US/hogan1 364.htm

Clark County Prosecuting Attorney (2014b). William L. Rousan. *ClarkProsecutor.org*. www.clarkprosecutor.org/html/death/US/rousan1 377.htm

Cooney, M., & Phillips, S. (2013). With God on one's side: The social geometry of death row apologies. *Sociological Forum, 28*(1), 159–178. https://doi.org/10.1111/socf.12007

Creo, R. A. (2016). Final moments. *Alternatives, 34*(5), 70–72. https://doi.org/10.1002/alt.21636

Death Penalty Information Center (2023). *Execution database*. https://deathpenaltyinfo.org/executions/execution-database?sort=dateStr ing/desc

Eaton, J. (2014). Honor on death row: Apology, remorse, and the culture of honor in the U.S. South. *SAGE Open, 4*, 1–9. https://doi.org/10.1177/2158244014529777

Eaton, J., & Roul, K. (2023). *Linguistic analysis of remorse in death row last statements*. Unpublished data.

Eaton, J., & Theuer, A. (2009). Apology and remorse in the last statements of death row prisoners. *Justice Quarterly, 26*(2), 327–347. https://doi.org/10.1080/07418820802245078

Exline, J. J., & Baumeister, R. F. (2000). Expressing forgiveness and repentance: Benefits and barriers. In M. E. McCullough, K. I. Pargament & C. E. Thoresen (Eds.), *The psychology of forgiveness* (pp. 133–155). Guilford.

Foley, S. R., & Kelly, B. D. (2018). Forgiveness, spirituality and love: Thematic analysis of last statements from Death Row, Texas (2002–17). *QJM: An International Journal of Medicine, 111*(6), 399–403. https://doi.org/10.1093/qjmed/hcy062

Goranson, A., Ritter, R. S., Waytz, A., Norton, M. I., & Gray, K. (2017). Dying is unexpectedly positive. *Psychological Science, 28*(7), 988–999. https://doi.org/10.1177/0956797617701186

Greenberg, J., Pyszczynski, T., Solomon, S. (1986). The causes and consequences of a need for self-esteem: A terror management theory. In R.F. Baumeister (Ed.), *Public Self and Private Self. Springer Series in Social Psychology* (pp. 189–212). Springer. https://doi.org/10.1007/978-1-4613-9564-5_10

Heflick, N. A. (2005). Sentenced to die: Last statements and dying on death row. *Omega, 51*(4), 323–336. https://doi.org/10.2190/96X8-FLUT-TCLH-EL71

Hirschmüller, S., & Egloff, B. (2016). Positive emotional language in the final words spoken directly before execution. *Frontiers in Psychology, 6*(1985), 1–10. https://doi.org/10.3389/fpsyg.2015.01985

Johnson, R. (1979). Under sentence of death: The psychology of death row confinement. *Law and Psychology Review, 5*, 141–192.

Kashdan, T. B., DeWall, C. N., Schurtz, D. R., Deckman, T., Lykins, E. L. B., Evans, D. R., McKenzie, J., Segerstrom, S. C., Gailliot, M. T., & Brown, K. W. (2014). More than words: Contemplating death enhances positive emotional word use. *Personality and Individual Differences, 71*, 171–175. https://doi.org/10.1016/j.paid.2014.07.035

Meinig, D. W. (2010). *Imperial Texas: An interpretive essay in cultural geography*. University of Texas Press.

Orenstein, A. (2010). Her last words: Dying declarations and modern confrontation jurisprudence. *University of Illinois Law Review, 5*, 1411–1460.

Pennebaker, J. W., Boyd, R. L., Booth, R. J., Ashokkumar, A., & Francis, M. E. (2022). *Linguistic inquiry and word count: LIWC-22*. Pennebaker Conglomerates. www.liwc.app

Prejean, H. (1994). *Dead man walking*. Vintage Press.

Prosecuting Attorney of Clark County (2023). *The death penalty*. www.clarkprosecutor.org/html/death/usexecute.htm

Rice, S. K., Dirks, D., & Exline, J. J. (2009). Of guilt, defiance, and repentance: Evidence from the Texas death chamber. *Justice Quarterly, 26*(2), 295–326. https://doi.org/10.1080/07418820802178063

Schuck, A. R., & Ward, J. (2008). Dealing with the inevitable: Strategies of self-presentation and meaning construction in the final statements of inmates on Texas death row. *Discourse & Society, 19*(1), 43–62. https://doi.org/10.1177/0957926507083687

Smith, R. A. (2020). Race, ethnicity, and the functional use of religion when faced with imminent death. *Religions, 11*(10), 77–95. https//doi.org/10.3390/rel11100500

Texas Department of Criminal Justice (1993). *Death row informa-tion: Inmate information.* www.tdcj.texas.gov/death_row/dr_info/hererr
aleonellast.html

Texas Department of Criminal Justice (1995). *Death row informa-tion: Inmate information.* www.tdcj.texas.gov/death_row/dr_info/john
soncarllast.html

Texas Department of Criminal Justice (2005). *Death row informa-tion: Inmate information.* www.tdcj.texas.gov/death_row/dr_info/rob
ertsdouglaslast.html

Texas Department of Criminal Justice (2006). *Death row informa-tion: Inmate information.* www.tdcj.texas.gov/death_row/dr_info/titsw
orthtimothylast.html

Texas Department of Criminal Justice (2011). *Death row informa-tion: Inmate information.* www.tdcj.texas.gov/death_row/dr_info/hall
michaellast.html

Texas Department of Criminal Justice (2013). *Death row informa-tion: Inmate information.* www.tdcj.texas.gov/death_row/dr_info/lewi
srickeylast.html

Texas Department of Criminal Justice (2017). *Death row informa-tion: Inmate information.* www.tdcj.texas.gov/death_row/dr_info/big
byjameslast.html

Texas Department of Criminal Justice (2023). *Death row informa-tion: Executed inmates.* www.tdcj.texas.gov/death_row/dr_executed_of
fenders.html

Upton, M. A., Carwile, T. M., & Brown, K. S. (2017). In their own
words: A qualitative exploration of last statements of capital punish-ment inmates in the State of Missouri, 1995–2011. *OMEGA-Journal
of Death and Dying, 75*(4), 376–394. https://doi.org/10.1177/003022281
6652972

Vollum, S., & Longmire, D. R. (2009). Giving voice to the dead: Last
statements of the condemned. *Contemporary Justice Review, 12*(1), 5–26. https://doi.org/10.1080/10282580802681576

Warren, A., & Jackson, C. A. (2022, December 14). Loden pronounced
dead at 6:12 p.m., coroner states. *WLBT.com.* www.wlbt.com/2022/12/
14/thomas-loden-jr-be-executed-parchman-wednesday-evening/

4 The forgiving victim?

Evidence from their statements to the media

I think he was very sincere. I could tell by the way he said it.
I wish I could have told him that I forgave him a long time
ago. I have prayed for him to find peace.

(victim's sister, cited in Johnson, 2009)

In 2009, after witnessing the execution of the person who murdered
their sister, this individual spoke to the press who were gathered
outside the prison. Jack Trawick, whose last statement appears at
the beginning of Chapter 3, had just apologized to the families
of his victims and asked for their forgiveness. She accepted his
apology. She appears to have already forgiven him and wished she
could have told him that.

In Chapter 3 we saw that, in their final statements before being
executed, 30% of the inmates offered an apology to their victim's
family members. How are these apologies received by the family
members? We know that apologies can be generally effective at
resolving, or at least reducing, the negative effects of conflict, but
what about when the transgressor is on death row and the person
affected by that transgression is about to witness their execution?
This is a very different context than a simple disagreement between
friends, so we cannot assume that the apology–forgiveness relationship is the same. In the case earlier, the apology was accepted.
However, as the research described in this chapter will show, this
response is not necessarily typical. Often when family members
witness executions their responses are more complex than this.

DOI: 10.4324/9781003384946-4

The effect of homicide on survivors

Victims of crime are a large, diverse group. While many countries, including Canada, the United Kingdom, and the United States, define what a victim is in the same way – as someone who has suffered physical, mental, or emotional harm or economic loss as the result of a crime – there are many ways to be victimized. Physical harm can range from a light slap to a severe physical assault with life-changing injuries; mental or emotional harm could range from a minor betrayal to an abusive and threatening spouse; and economic loss could be small, such as having some change from your car stolen, to identity theft that causes you to lose your life's savings. In addition to the wide range of ways to be victimized, there is also a wide range of reactions to this victimization. Two victims might respond very differently to the same crime, and this could depend on factors such as their physical and mental state prior to the crime, their prior history of victimization, their current financial and economic situation, and their personality (Randa & Reyns, 2020).

The effects of crime are not limited to the person who committed the crime and the person who was the victim of the crime. Each of those individuals has family, friends, and other loved ones who may be impacted by the crime, whether it's the added emotional or physical support the victim might need, the shame of being the family member of an offender, or the added time and stress involved in navigating the criminal justice system. When the crime committed is homicide the effects can be even worse for those close to the victim. In addition to the grief and sadness that can be experienced after losing a loved one to non-violent bereavement, losing a loved one to homicide comes with the additional burden of managing feelings of intense anger, questions about fairness and justice, and the necessity of interacting with the justice system and the media (Armour, 2002; Burton & Tewksbury, 2013). These effects are similar to what a direct victim of a crime might experience, and one could make the case that having a loved one taken from you is itself a crime. Some victim's rights regulations formally recognize this; for example, the *Code of Practice for Victims of Crime in England and Wales* specifies that a victim can be "a close relative (or a nominated family spokesperson) of a person whose death was directly caused by a criminal offence" (Ministry of

Justice, 2020, p. 3). People whose lives are negatively impacted by the homicide of a family member or close friend are often referred to as "covictims" (Armour, 2002) or "secondary victims" (Hodgkinson et al., 2009). Because "secondary victimization" is sometimes used to refer to the negative effects that victims themselves experience as they navigate the criminal justice system (e.g., Williams, 1984), we'll use the term "covictims."

Emotional and physical effects

The anger, grief, and frustration experienced by covictims following the murder of a loved one can be intense. Interviews and clinical studies with covictims have shown that they often suffer from prolonged negative outcomes such as post-traumatic stress disorder, chronic grief, and depression (Alves-Costa et al., 2021; Boelen et al., 2015; Rheingold et al., 2015; van Denderen et al., 2018). The crime might have other significant psychological outcomes, such as changing how they view themselves or making them reassess their long-held worldviews (Discola, 2021; Kenney, 2002) and causing them to question, or even abandon, their faith (Sprang et al., 1989). This psychological suffering can also lead to, and be exacerbated by, behavioural and physical outcomes such as nightmares and insomnia, addiction issues, and physical illness (King, 2004; Rando, 1993).

In addition to the emotional and physical effects of the crime, the experiences of covictims also differ from those of other bereaved people because of their involvement with the criminal justice system. Ironically, if the offender has been given a death sentence covictims' involvement with the justice system is even more involved and lengthy (Burton & Tewksbury, 2013). With a death sentence comes longer trials and more appeals. These continuous interactions with the justice system can prevent covictims from moving on from the event. As one covictims notes, "every time that lawyer calls about the appeal, it's like my brother is being murdered again. The pain just floods back in" (King, 2004, p. 201). Covictims report dissatisfaction with many aspects of their involvement with the justice system, including a lack of clear information, not receiving information and notifications of upcoming court dates in a timely manner, long and repeated delays and cancellations, lack of respect or empathy, and having to relive the trauma during the trial (Reed & Caraballo, 2022).

Social effects

Covictims might also struggle socially, and they might not get the type of validation they need from others. Finding the best way to offer condolences and support for bereaved people can be difficult, and it might be especially hard when the loss is due to homicide. Well-meaning others might not know what to say, so they might either say something that is perceived as being insensitive (such as "it was meant to be"), or they might avoid the covictim. This can lead to social isolation at a time when covictims need support the most. As a woman who lost her sister to homicide noted,

> nobody who hasn't gone through this hell on earth can understand what we're going through. At first, people called and came by. They were real nice. Then it seemed like they were in a hurry for us to get over it.

> (King, 2004, p. 202)

There can also be stigma attached to losing a loved one to murder – people might assume that the victim somehow contributed to their death through engaging in illegal activity (Sharpe, 2015) or by otherwise not being an "ideal victim" (Christie, 1986). Others might blame the covictim for not doing enough to protect the victim, and so might the covictims themselves (King, 2004; Sharpe, 2015).

Covictim responses to the execution

The effects of homicide on covictims can be devastating, regardless of the context. However, capital cases are unique in one important way: The covictims have the opportunity to be present when the offender is executed. This gives them the chance to hear directly from the offender. As we saw in Chapter 3, some offenders do address the covictims, and often when they do they offer an apology. Given how devastating homicide can be for the survivors of the victims, how are these apologies received? And, more broadly, what might covictims feel after receiving (or not receiving) an apology and then witnessing the death of the offender? There is, of course, no "right" way for a covictim to react in this situation, but there are two concepts that seem particularly relevant here: forgiveness and closure (or lack thereof).

Forgiveness

Even though forgiveness can free up energy for more positive emotions (Ysseldyk et al., 2007), improve emotional well-being (Karremans et al., 2003), and lead to improved physical health (Witvliet et al., 2001), covictims may have valid reasons for not forgiving. Losing a loved one to homicide can be a life-changing, ongoing source of trauma, and it is easy to understand the anger that covictims might feel – toward the offender and perhaps also toward the criminal justice system. A death sentence for the offender might be a source of comfort for them, and after the execution they might feel relieved, vindicated, or even happy. Some covictims might find the thought of forgiveness to be completely unacceptable, especially if it is recommended by someone else too early in the process. Armour (2003) quotes a covictim's response to a chaplain who suggested that they should think about forgiveness: "anybody who has dealt with homicide for any period of time knows that forgiveness...doesn't come for a while. The thought doesn't even hit your head until you are ready for it" (p. 527).

Not all covictims feel this way, however. Some do not support the death penalty and do not want it to be applied in their case (King, 2003), and some even come to forgive the offender over time. Marietta Jaeger, for example, speaks eloquently about forgiving the man who murdered her daughter Susie: "Though I readily admit that initially I wanted to kill this man with my bare hands, by the time of the resolution of his crimes, I was convinced that my best and healthiest option was to forgive" (Jaeger, 1998, p. 14). Kate and Andy Grosmaire received international media attention when they forgave Conor McBride, the young man who murdered their daughter, Ann, and requested a drastically reduced sentence for him (Grosmaire & French, 2016). There are many more stories of people who have forgiven those who murdered a loved one. The Forgiveness Project (theforgivenessproject.com) attempts to normalize the idea of forgiveness by documenting and sharing stories of those who have forgiven seemingly unforgiveable crimes.

Within the broader criminal justice system there has been a movement to recognize that at least some victims are prepared to try to forgive their offenders, and that there are benefits to helping facilitate this. Restorative justice programmes provide opportunities for dialogue between victims and offenders, and although forgiveness is not the expressed purpose of this, it can be an outcome. Victims do not have to participate in restorative justice programmes, but many of them do, and studies show that they often do it specifically because they want an apology (Petrucci, 2002; Strang & Sherman, 2003). Some restorative justice programmes report rates of forgiveness in victims as high as 75% (Sherman et al., 2005). Although restorative justice has been less frequently used in cases of severe crime such as murder, there is some evidence that even the victims or covictims of these crimes are willing to, if not fully forgive offenders, at least see offenders as more human and stop being angry towards them (Umbreit et al., 1999). It must be noted that those victims and covictims who agree to participate in such programmes may be more prepared to forgive than those who choose not to participate, but the data still indicate that some victims are prepared to forgive their offenders.

In addition to restorative justice initiatives, direct interventions can be effective at helping to facilitate forgiveness (Freedman & Enright, 1996). There are also specific contextual and interpersonal factors that can affect whether covictims will be willing to forgive. For instance, the higher the degree of injustice they feel, the less they are likely to forgive (Gerlsma & Lugtmeyer, 2018). Although in the context of covictims of homicide the crime committed is the same, covictims may differ in their satisfaction with how the case was handled or resolved and their own perceptions of what constitutes justice (Randa & Reyns, 2020). Forgiveness can also be affected by the relationship between the covictim and the offender. It might be relatively straightforward to refuse to forgive a stranger for murdering a loved one, but if the homicide was committed by a family member forgiveness can become more complicated. On one hand, forgiveness might be more possible because the perpetrator is someone who is known and loved, and thus it might be easier to have empathy for them (Yu et al., 2023). On the other hand, the sense of betrayal might be much stronger when the perpetrator is someone who was loved and trusted, making forgiveness less likely (Laughon et al., 2008). In a similar way, there is some evidence that it is easier to forgive when the covictim and perpetrator share the same cultural background (Discola, 2020), but this could also discourage forgiveness if the covictim felt that the offender had betrayed their cultural group. The covictim's religious beliefs can also affect the degree to which they are willing to forgive, in that many religions include forgiveness as a central teaching (Worthington, 1998). If a covictim belonged to a religion that encouraged forgiveness they might be more inclined to forgive the offender (Johnson et al., 2023). However, another important factor in forgiveness is the understanding that one has a choice in whether to forgive (Johnson et al., 2023). If a covictim felt obligated to offer forgiveness because of their religion, but they did not actually feel forgiveness towards the offender, this would not be considered "true" forgiveness.

Sometimes covictims might want to forgive but feel pressured to not forgive. Forgiveness is generally considered to be a virtue, and those who forgive are often seen in a positive light (Seligman & Csikszentmihalyi, 2000). However, when a covictim chooses to forgive the person who murdered their loved one, their decision can invite ambivalent responses from others, who may evaluate the "forgivability" of the event differently from the victim (Watanabe & Laurent, 2020). Some covictims have felt afraid to speak out about their true feelings for fear of offending or hurting the feelings of family members who might not agree with them (Barrile, 2015; King, 2003). Even people who have nothing to do with the crime or the people involved might have strong feelings about forgiveness. Third parties – people who are not directly involved in the situation – are often more critical and less forgiving than victims are towards an offender and are less likely to see the act of forgiveness as beneficial for the victim (Cooney et al., 2011). This "third-party forgiveness effect" (Green et al., 2008) can result in a division between covictims who want to forgive and third parties who believe that withholding forgiveness from an offender is a more appropriate response. These judgements can be detrimental to covictims, who may want to forgive the transgressor but are reluctant to do so publicly because they fear they will be judged negatively. Wilma Derksen, who forgave the person who murdered her daughter in Winnipeg in 1984, explains the harm that public judgement can cause: "At times it was incredibly tough. People said we couldn't have loved Candace because we forgave [her murderer]" (Derksen, 2019). Even if third parties might be reluctant to outwardly criticize a covictim for choosing to forgive, they often disagree with the decision to forgive severe crimes (Eaton et al., 2022). Rather than providing the validation and support that covictims need, this type of reaction can make them feel even more victimized (Montada, 1994; Orth, 2002). In speaking of the public reaction to her after she forgave the suicide bomber who staged an attack at an Ariana Grande concert at the Manchester Arena in 2017 where her son was killed, Figen Murray says,

> I went public with my forgiveness early on because I felt it was such an important message but I have been very much the odd one out among the other bereaved families and I sense their bewilderment about my forgiveness. I often fear that people see me as naïve and soft, but I am neither.
>
> (Murray, 2023)

Closure

Another term that is commonly used in relation to capital punishment is closure. In a popular sense, closure refers to the end of some type of suffering, such as what might be desired upon the death of a loved one or the end of a relationship. It is often used in the context of victims, to describe their need to have some type of finality, ending, or completion to the pain the crime has caused them (Bandes, 2009). Closure is a particularly well-used term in the context of the death penalty. Opinion polls suggest that public support for the death penalty comes, at least in part, from the belief that it provides closure to the family members of victims (Zimring, 2004). Policymakers have also used this argument to justify imposing the death penalty (Armour & Umbreit, 2007; Bandes, 2021; Berns, 2009; Kanwar, 2001). The practice of allowing family members of victims (i.e., covictims) to attend executions is rooted in the belief that witnessing the death of the offender will "contribute to the healing process" (Texas Department of Criminal Justice, 2023). Covictims themselves often refer to closure when they speak of their hopes for the outcome of the execution.

Given the popularity of the notion of closure and its obvious relevance to covictims, it is surprising that there is very little empirical research in this area. In addition, the little research that has been done is inconclusive. Acker and Karp (2006), in their collection of interviews and essays about covictim perspectives on the death penalty, find little evidence of closure in covictims.

Rather, a common sentiment throughout this work is that covictims feel that there is no such thing as closure because their loved one cannot be brought back. Similarly, Saco and Dirks (2018), in interviews with experts on homicide survivorship (many of whom were themselves survivors), found that most of their respondents did not agree with the notion of closure, claiming it "did not exist for survivors" (p. 841). Some claimed that the use of the word was insensitive, or even offensive, and one participant said, "you cause a riot in a meeting of murder victims [survivors] if you talk about closure, so never say the 'C' word" (Saco & Dirks, 2018, p. 841). In contrast, Gross and Matheson (2003) and Vollum and Longmire (2007) conducted content analyses of the statements that covictims made to the press following the execution and both concluded that closure was a predominant theme, with many covictims reporting a sense of closure. The conflicting findings between the interviews and the content analyses may be due, at least in part, to the differing methodologies that were used in the studies. They may also be due to the fact that there is no clear definition of what closure actually means (Bandes, 2009; Zimring, 2004). Covictims may have varying perceptions of what closure is, which means that covictims with very similar feelings may label these feelings quite differently. For example, two covictims may express relief that an offender has been punished (either through execution of some other means), but one may label that relief as closure, while the other may report that they feel no closure.

The research study

Overview

Current attitudes about covictims and the death penalty seem to be based on general assumptions that (a) covictims are not forgiving, and (b) the execution of the offender will bring them closure. Some of the research offers support for this (e.g., Gross & Matheson, 2003; Vollum & Longmire, 2007) and some does not (e.g., Eaton & Christensen, 2014; Saco & Dirks, 2018; Umbreit et al., 1999). Covictims may have varied and complicated feelings about the death penalty. We would not expect them to feel the same as other covictims – there may be different attitudes and/or disagreements even within families – nor would we expect individuals to feel the same way over time. Thus, there is no "typical" covictim response to the execution of the person who murdered their loved one. The rest of this chapter describes research that focuses on the covictims. Acknowledging that no two covictims will experience their loss in exactly the same way, this research study does not seek to find definitive answers about whether covictims forgive or find closure. However, it does aim to understand how they talk about these concepts after the execution. In the United States, when an offender is executed, the family members (and sometimes close friends) of their victims are permitted to witness the execution. During the execution they have no direct contact with the offender; they watch from a room with a window that looks into the execution chamber. There is a microphone in the execution chamber that enables them to hear the offender's last words, but the offender typically cannot hear them. Where possible, the supporters of the offender and the supporters of the victim are kept separate. After the execution, the covictims are given the opportunity to speak with the media. These statements are a rich source of data, in that they can shed some light on how the covictims feel immediately after witnessing the death of the person who killed their loved one.

The data

The data for this study are the words of the covictims, found in news articles written about the execution. Prior research has used similar data and methods, and this study builds on that research. Vollum and Longmire (2007) examined 320 executions between 1982 and 2004, but only from Texas. Two other studies used data from the entire United States: Gross and Matheson (2003) examined 100 executions between 2001 and 2002 and Eaton and Christensen (2014) examined 679 executions between 2000 and 2011. Building on this prior research, this study uses data from 960 executions from January 2000 to December 2022, from the entire United States. There was a practical reason for not including the executions between 1976 (when the death penalty was reinstated) and 1999 – it's difficult to find online news reports prior to 2000. Also, covictims have not always been allowed to witness executions; for example, Texas only began allowing them to attend

Table 4.1 Covictim attendance at executions

	Total	Statement	No statement
Covictim(s) in attendance	596 (62.1%)	477 (80%)	119 (20%)
Covictim(s) not in attendance	104 (10.8%)		
Unknown	260 (27.1%)		
Total	960		

in 1996. Limiting the data collection to executions that took place after 1999 likely only excludes a small number of covictims who witnessed the execution.

Information about the covictims and their statements to the media was collected by searching for news articles providing information about each execution in the United States that had occurred between January 2000 and December 2022. Not all articles mentioned the victims, but for those that did, information was recorded as to (a) whether any covictims had attended the execution, (b) whether they made a statement to the press immediately following the execution, and (c) what they said in their statement.

Table 4.1 shows the breakdown of how many of the executions included covictims as witnesses and how many made a statement to the media afterwards. Interestingly, 62% of the executions were witnessed by at least one covictim. This is likely a conservative estimate of how many executions actually were witnessed by covictims because for 27% of the executions we found no mention of whether covictims were present or not. Of the executions where covictims were definitely present, we found covictim statements for 80% of them. In the remaining 20% of cases covictims either refused to make a public statement or there was no mention of whether a covictim made a statement or not.

Findings

Content analysis

Using a similar strategy as with the inmates last statements, described in Chapter 3, we conducted a content analysis of the statements made by covictims to the media. In an attempt to focus solely on the voice of the covictims, we only analysed covictim comments that were direct quotes. For example, if the media report said that a covictim was angry but did not provide a quote of them actually *saying* they were angry it was not included in the analysis. This was an attempt to reduce the bias that might arise from a reporter inaccurately interpreting how their interviewee might feel, but it also eliminated some data from the analysis.

The content analysis focused on specific themes. First, we looked for comments related to forgiveness and closure. We also included some of the themes identified in prior research, to see if we could replicate that research using the longer time frame. These themes included justice, frustration with the process, revenge, disappointment, and compassion/sympathy for the offender's family. Table 4.2 shows the number of statements to the press containing each variable.

Forgiveness. Not surprisingly, forgiveness was not mentioned by covictims very often: Only about 10% specifically said that they had forgiven or potentially could forgive the offender and almost 5% said they would never forgive the offender. Their forgiveness was not necessarily related to whether the inmate apologized. If they had chosen to forgive before the execution, in some cases it did not seem to matter whether the inmate offered an apology or not. One family explicitly said that they forgave the offender despite the fact that he did not apologize (Thompson, 2022).

Table 4.2 Frequency of coded variables

Variable	Total
Forgiveness	
Yes/maybe	50 (10.5%)
No/never	23 (4.8%)
Closure	
Yes/maybe	77 (16.1%)
No/never/impossible	75 (15.7%)
Implied closure	55 (11.5%)
Justice	178 (37.2%)
Frustration with process	174 (36.4%)
Revenge	113 (23.6%)
Disappointment	25 (12.1%)
Compassion	56 (11.7%)

Others who forgave were clear about separating forgiveness from justice. In the example below, the covictim specifies that just because they forgave the inmate does not mean he should not be punished for the crime:

> He asked for forgiveness and I forgive him, but he had to pay the consequences.
>
> (survivor, cited in Graczyk, 2012)

Closure. Many covictims mentioned closure (more than one-third of them), but not always in a positive way. Of those who used the word "closure" specifically, only about half indicated that they had or could imagine getting closure; the other half said they did not get closure and/or that closure was impossible. For those who said they got closure, they sometimes mentioned that it was the reason they attended the execution:

> I came here today to find a little bit of closure. I know this won't bring him back, but I do feel like I got a sense of closure today.
>
> (victim's sister, cited in Edwards, 2009)

For those who said they did not feel that the execution gave them closure, some simply said that closure was not possible:

> I don't have no closure. And him being put to death, is not going to be closure either because then we'll never know why.
>
> (victim's sister, cited in Marcus & Massie, 2021)

Another 11.5% didn't use the word "closure," but used similar words or phrases like "ending," "last chapter."

Justice. The most common theme (mentioned by 37% of the covictims) was justice, in that they specifically said that "justice had been served" or a similar sentiment. It is possible that justice was mentioned so frequently because covictims are often specifically asked by members of the press if they felt that justice had been served.

Frustration with the process. The second-most common theme (mentioned by 36% of the covictims) was frustration with the justice process. Their frustration mainly stemmed from the length of time it had taken between the offender being sentenced and the actual execution. Offenders are on death row for an average of

13.5 years, so this complaint is not unjustified. Many commented that they had been waiting a long time for the execution to happen:

> Today marks final justice for our daughter Vicki Lynne. Our family has waited 37 years, eight months and 22 days for this day to come.
>
> (victim's mother, cited in Koenig, 2022)

Others were not only frustrated with how long it took but also by the process itself:

> It is glaringly apparent that there is something fundamentally flawed with a justice system that takes over 32 years to bring to justice a pedophile who confessed to kidnapping and murdering a 10-year-old girl...For the last 12,000 days, there have been arguments about pieces of paper that have no bearing on the facts of this case.
>
> (victim's brother, cited in Sullivan, 2013)

Others pointed out that the inmate had been on death row longer than their loved one had been alive:

> Twenty-five years ago, Susan's life was suddenly and brutally extinguished. We have grieved for her longer than she was with us.
>
> (victim's sister, cited in Kitching, 2018)

Revenge. Another common theme was revenge, with 23.6% of covictims expressing some type of vengeful feeling towards the offender. Sometimes this was in the form of a statement that the offender got what he/she deserved. Other times it came as a criticism that the execution process was too humane compared to how their loved one died.

> This man conducted a horrific murder and you guys are going, let's worry about the drugs. Why didn't they give him a bullet, why didn't we give him Drano?
>
> (victim's family member, cited in Berman, 2014)

> Tonight we watched the quiet, peaceful death of Worthington, who murdered our Mindy. His peaceful death was in stark

contrast to the violent and painful death that Mindy suffered at his hands.

(victim's father, cited in Stebbings, 2014)

Others showed anger towards the offender, expressing satisfaction that he will "burn in hell":

Danny Paul Bible is as vile and evil a person that has ever drawn breath. We are glad to have witnessed him draw his last breath. I know he will burn in hell for eternity.

(victim's brother, cited in Chavez, 2018)

Disappointment. Some came away from the execution disappointed in the offender's final words. Most often this was because they were hoping for an apology but did not receive one:

You just wanted to hear him say, "I am sorry for what I did," and you never heard that. He was always so smug about getting away with it.

(victim's family member, cited in Sims, 2009)

Compassion/sympathy for the offender's family. In addition to these mostly negative themes, covictims sometimes showed empathy and compassion towards the offender and his/her family, with almost 12% expressing their sympathy towards the offender's family. Some struggled with the idea that, while they may have felt the execution was warranted, they understood that the offender's family would suffer:

On one hand, I felt we were finally going to get justice, but on the other, I felt sad for your family. They are now going to go through the pain we experienced.

(victim's sister, cited in Allen, 2021)

Predictors of forgiveness

The number of covictims who expressed forgiveness immediately after witnessing the execution was fairly low, and in many cases it seemed as though the covictims had already decided to forgive the offender before the execution. In order to test whether any variables

Table 4.3 Predictors of forgiveness

Predictor	β	SE β	Wald's χ^2	df	p	Odds ratio
Offender variables						
Apology	−.37	.49	.58	1	.45	.69
Responsibility	−.55	.52	1.15	1	.29	.58
Sincerity	.91	.49	3.38	1	.07	2.47
Ask for forgiveness	.95	.45	4.44	1	.04	2.60
Covictim variables						
Closure	.08	.51	.03	1	.87	1.09
Justice	−.04	.40	.01	1	.91	.96
Revenge	−.76	.57	1.74	1	.19	.47
Disappointment	−.28	.78	.13	1	.72	.75
Accept apology	1.51	.52	8.63	1	.003	4.54
Constant	−2.64	.36	52.44	1	<.001	.07

were able to reliably predict whether a covictim would forgive, a logistic regression, similar to the one in Chapter 3, was conducted. Two sets of predictor variables were included: Those related to the offender's last statement (whether they made an apology, took responsibility, seemed sincere, and asked for forgiveness) and variables in the covictims' statements to the press (whether they got closure, felt that justice was served, made vengeful comments, were disappointed with the offender's last words, and whether they accepted the offender's apology). Covictim forgiveness was the outcome variable.

Table 4.3 shows the results of the logistic regression. The overall model was significant, meaning that as a group, the variables were able to predict whether covictims would forgive or not. The statistic for this overall test of the model is the chi-square test: χ^2 (9, $N = 477) = 25.13, p = .003$. The model as a whole explained between 7% (Cox and Snell R square) and 14% (Nagelkerke R square) of the variance in forgiveness, and correctly classified 89.8% of cases. Although this model is significant, the low percentages for the Cox and Snell R square and the Nalelkerke R square indicate that it does not do a good job of explaining why covictims forgive. Only two variables significantly predict whether the covictim will forgive (those with values less than .05 in the *p* column): whether the offender asked for forgiveness and whether the covictim said they had accepted the offender's apology. Whether the offender made an apology or took responsibility in their final statement did not predict whether the covictim would forgive.

What statements to the media tell us about covictims

As in our prior research analysing covictims' statements to the media after witnessing the execution (Eaton & Christensen, 2014), they generally did not report that they forgave the offender. For the approximately 10% who did say they either forgave or could imagine forgiving in the future, it did not appear that their decision to forgive was directly because of the offender's death-bed apology. From their statements to the media it seemed that they had already made a decision about forgiveness prior to attending the execution. The logistic regression provided further evidence of this, as it showed that offender apology did not significantly predict covictim forgiveness. While this retrospective data cannot tell us anything about causality, it seems more likely that covictims' decisions to forgive were based on their own internal processes than about the words of the offender during the execution.

While one-third of covictims used the word "closure" in their statements to the media, they were divided on whether the death of the offender provided it or not. Half of those who mentioned closure said they either got it or could imagine having it in the future, and half said they did not get it and never would. This does not support the arguments suggesting that the death penalty is necessary because it brings covictims closure. Interpreting this theme in their statements was complicated by the fact that covictims may have had different ideas about what closure means. Some of them used the word closure, but some used similar words such as "ending" or phrases such as "closing a chapter." The term "closure" implies an end to suffering, or the arrival of some type of peace. Some covictims were very clear that the pain of the loss would never go away, but they also mentioned that the execution brought them closure. It's possible that those who said they would never get closure were defining closure as an end to the pain, whereas those who said they got closure were defining it as a final step in the process, or an ending. These findings support the argument that closure is challenging to study because no one seems to agree on what it is (Bandes, 2009; Zimring, 2004).

Rather than forgiveness and closure, covictims often expressed feelings of anger and revenge, and indicated that the execution was the appropriate punishment for the offender (i.e., that "justice had been served"). Sometimes their anger was directed at the justice process itself. They spoke of how many years it had been since their loved one had been murdered, and how stressful the seemingly endless process of appeals and requests for stays of execution had been for them. Some also displayed anger toward the offender and noted that the treatment of the offender during the execution was more humane than the treatment of their loved one at the hands of the offender. Others mentioned wanting to get revenge on the offender themselves. While it is understandable why covictims might feel this way, the long-term effects of these types of negative feelings can be devastating – homicide survivors who report feelings of vengeance are more likely to experience symptoms of post-traumatic stress disorder and complicated grief (van Denderen et al., 2018). In addition, studies show that although revenge might feel good in the short-term, these positive effects tend to be short-lived (Carlsmith et al., 2008). When individuals take revenge, it ultimately tends to increase rather than decrease vengeful feelings (Bushman, 2002). Therefore, if covictims see their attendance at the execution as a way of exacting revenge on the offender, this might not be good for them in the long run. This is not to suggest that having an offender be punished for their crime is not good for the victim, but harsher punishments do not necessarily bring more satisfaction (Orth, 2004). Victims tend to report more satisfaction with punishment when the offender also shows signs of reformation (Hechler et al., 2023), but there is little opportunity for behaviour change or reform on death row.

Some covictims seemed to feel conflicted about the execution. Even if they felt the execution was justified, just over 10% expressed sympathy for the offender's family, acknowledging that they too were losing a loved one. For many covictims, this might have been the first time they had seen the offender's family. Where possible, the witnesses for the offender and the witnesses for the victim are generally kept separate during the execution, but even just seeing them might have helped covictims see them as another family that was grieving the loss of a loved one.

The analysis of covictims' statements to the media after witnessing the execution does not provide convincing evidence that they benefit from their involvement in this stage of the justice process, and it might even do them more harm than good. Although there are limits to how much their relatively brief statements to the media can tell us about the long-term effects of the execution on covictims (see below), these findings suggest that covictims are not universally better off because the offender was executed.

The limitations of using statements to the media as a data source

What we know about covictims' feelings about the death penalty, and the execution specifically, comes from what they are willing to share. Some covictims wish to speak about their experience, but some do not. Therefore, any study examining the effects of executions on the survivors is subject to sampling bias. If we base our conclusions about covictims' feelings about the death penalty solely on the comments of those individuals who are willing to be interviewed, then we run the risk of incorrectly attributing these same feelings to those who choose *not* to share their stories. It is important to remember that the voices of those who choose to be silent are not represented in any study of how crime affects victims and covictims (Groger et al., 1999).

This study of covictims' statements to the press is subject to sampling bias because some subsets of covictims are not represented – those who we know did not attend the execution and those for whom no information was available about whether they attended or not. For the just over 10% who we know did not attend the execution, we don't know their reasons for not attending – maybe they didn't want to, but maybe they wanted to but couldn't, for financial, health, or other reasons. If they were not there by choice, it might have been because they didn't feel the need to – maybe they had already forgiven, or felt they had closure, or were simply against the death penalty – but it could also have been that they had no intention of forgiving the offender so they did not want to hear the offender's last words, or they were too angry or upset to attend.

There are another 27% about whom we have no information because no mention of covictims was made in the media coverage of the execution. It is impossible to know if they attended the execution and made a statement that was not reported, they attended the execution but declined to make a statement, or if they did not attend. Generally, if there was anything sensational about the offender (for example, if he/she was not from the United States, if there was a question about his/her guilt, if he/she had high-profile or celebrity supporters) the media tended to report on this and not mention the victims at all. This source of bias in reporting on capital punishment has been noted by others as well (Hochstetler, 2001). Some journalists (who sometimes covered multiple executions) seemed more likely than others to mention victims in their coverage of executions, which might have resulted in underrepresentation of victim narratives from certain geographical areas. This was less of an issue when there were multiple sources of media coverage, but this was not always the case, especially with the earlier executions.

Even if the media did report on the covictims, there is no way of knowing if they did so accurately. We did not want to rely on the reporter's interpretation of how the covictim felt, so we only used direct quotes from the covictims in the analysis. This is not foolproof, however. While this may have limited the extent to which the data contained the reporters' subjective take on what the covictims said, there is no way to verify that the covictims actually made these statements. Thus, this dataset is subject to media bias and error.

Another important consideration with these data is that the covictims' statements were recorded at one point in time, right after they had witnessed a person be executed. Even if they felt relief or justice at the time and were completely in support of the death penalty, this must have been a surreal, and potentially very difficult, thing for them to witness. Some of them may have struggled to express their true feelings, or even to fully understand how they were feeling, immediately afterwards. While their statements to the media may have been an indicator of their true feelings at the time, it's impossible to know. They may have been nervous in front of the media, or they may have censored what they wanted to say, or they may have been unable to think clearly after an emotionally charged day. This dataset also only represents their thoughts immediately after witnessing the execution. We do not know if they felt the same way one week, one month, one year, or even five years after the execution. Knowing how their feelings change over time would add an important dimension to our understanding. Interviews conducted at different stages of the process might help us learn about how their feelings might change over time, but sampling bias would still be an issue, as not everyone would agree to be interviewed.

This dataset is, without question, flawed. However, that does not mean that we should discount these findings. It is true that about one-quarter of the data were missing, but that does not mean that the findings based on the other three-quarters are not valid. To be sure, we cannot say that they apply to all covictims, but we can say that they apply to many. When combined with studies using different methods (i.e., interviews), they help paint a more detailed picture of how covictims feel about the death penalty.

References

Acker, J. R., & Karp, D. R. (2006). *Wounds that do not bind: Victim-based perspectives on the death penalty.* Carolina Academic Press.

Allen, J. (2021, January 29). At the funeral of man executed by U.S., family prays it is the last of its kind. *Reuters.* www.reuters.com/article/us-usa-executions-funeral-idUSKBN29Z04B

Alves-Costa, F., Hamilton-Giachritsis, C., Christie, H., van Denderen, M., & Halligan, S. (2021). Psychological interventions for individuals bereaved by homicide: A systematic review. *Trauma, Violence, & Abuse, 22*(4), 793–803. https://doi.org/10.1177/1524838019881716

Armour, M. P. (2002). Experiences of covictims of homicide: Implications for research and practice. *Trauma, Violence, & Abuse, 3*(2), 109–124. https://doi.org/10.1177/15248380020032002

Armour, M. P. (2003). Meaning making in the aftermath of homicide. *Death studies, 27*(6), 519–540. https://doi.org/10.1080/07481180302884

Armour, M. P., & Umbreit, M. S. (2007). Ultimate penal sanction and closure for survivors of homicide victims. *Marquette Law Review, 91*(1), 381–424.

Bandes, S. A. (2009). Victims, closure, and the sociology of emotion. *Law & Contemporary Problems, 72*, 1–26.

Bandes, S. A. (2021). Closure in the criminal courtroom: The birth and strange career of an emotion. In S. A. Bandes, J. L. Madeira, K. D. Temple, & E. K. White (Eds.), *Research Handbook on Law and Emotion* (pp. 102–118). Edward Elgar Publishing.

Barrile, L. G. (2015). I forgive you, but you must die: Murder victim family members, the death penalty, and restorative justice. *Victims & Offenders, 10*(3), 239–269. https://doi.org/10.1080/15564886.2014.925022

Berman, M. (2014, July 24). Arizona execution lasts nearly two hours; lawyer says Joseph Wood was 'gasping and struggling to breathe'; The execution of Joseph Wood III took nearly two hours, prompting criticism and an official review. *The Washington Post.* www.washingtonp ost.com/news/post-nation/wp/2014/07/23/arizona-supreme-court-stays-planned-execution/

Berns, N. (2009). Contesting the victim card: Closure disclosure and emotion in death penalty rhetoric. *The Sociological Quarterly, 50,* 383–406. https://doi.org/10.1111/j.1533-8525.2009.01145.x

Boelen, P. A., de Keijser, J., & Smid, G. (2015). Cognitive-behavioral variables mediate the impact of violent loss on post-loss psychopathology. *Psychological Trauma: Theory, Research, Practice, and Policy, 7*(4), 382–390. https://doi.org/10.1037/tra0000018

Burton, C., & Tewksbury, R. (2013). How families of murder victims feel following the execution of their loved one's murderer: A content analysis of newspaper reports of executions from 2006–2011. *Journal of Qualitative Criminal Justice & Criminology, 1*(1), 1–25. https://doi.org/10.21428/88de04a1.06ddd37a

Bushman, B. J. (2002). Does venting anger feed or extinguish the flame? Catharsis, rumination, distraction, anger, and aggressive responding. *Personality and Social Psychology Bulletin, 28*(6), 724–731. https://doi.org/10.1177/0146167202289002

Carlsmith, K. M., Wilson, T. D., & Gilbert, D. T. (2008). The paradoxical consequences of revenge. *Journal of Personality and Social Psychology, 95*(6), 1316–1324. https://doi.org/10.1037/a0012165

Chavez, N. (2018, June 29). Texas 'ice pick killer' executed with lethal injection wanted a firing squad or gas death. *CNN.com.* www.cnn.com/2018/06/28/us/texas-danny-bible-execution/index.html

Christie, N. (1986). The ideal victim. In E. A. Fattah (Ed.), *From crime policy to victim policy* (pp. 17–30). Macmillan.

Cooney, A., Allan, A., Allan, M. M., McKillop, D., & Drake, D. G. (2011). The forgiveness process in primary and secondary victims of violent and sexual offences. *Australian Journal of Psychology, 63*(2), 107–118. https://doi.org/10.1111/j.1742-9536.2011.00012.x

Derksen, W. (2019). Wilma Derksen. *The Forgiveness Project.* www.thefor givenessproject.com/wilma-derksen

Discola, K. L. (2020). *Redefining murder, transforming emotion: An exploration of forgiveness after loss due to homicide.* Routledge.

Discola, K. L. (2021). Emerging narratives in the wake of homicide: Victim, survivor and transcender. *Journal of Victimology and Victim Justice, 3*(2), 202–218. https://doi.org/10.1177/2516606920972044

Eaton, J., & Christensen, T. (2014). Closure and its myths: Victims' families, the death penalty, and the closure argument. *International Review*

of Victimology, 20(3), 327–343. https://doi.org/10.1177/026975801
4537148

Eaton, J., Olenewa, J., & Norton, C. (2022). Judging "extreme" forgivers: How victims are perceived when they forgive the unforgivable. *International Review of Victimology, 28*(1), 33–51. https://doi.org/10.1177/02697580211028021

Edwards, K. (2009, January 21). Moore executed for 1994 murders. *The Huntsville Item.* www.itemonline.com/news/local_news/moore-execu
ted-for-1994-murders/article_9424a1d0-b3f7-5986-a4ef-d65d4b160
167.html

Freedman, S., & Enright, R. D. (1996). Forgiveness as an intervention goal with incest survivors. *Journal of Consulting and Clinical Psychology, 64,* 983–992. https://doi.org/10.1037/0022-006X.64.5.983

Gerlsma, C., & Lugtmeyer, V. (2018). Offense type as determinant of revenge and forgiveness after victimization: Adolescents' responses to injustice and aggression. *Journal of School Violence, 17*(1), 16–27. https://doi.org/10.1080/15388220.2016.1193741

Graczyk, M. (2012, April 26). Texas man executed for role in robbery-shooting. *Lubbock Avalanche-Journal.* www.lubbockonline.com/story/
news/state/2012/04/27/texas-man-executed-role-robbery-shooting/1516
1285007/

Green, J. D., Burnette, J. L., & Davis, J. L. (2008). Third-party forgiveness: (Not) forgiving your close other's betrayer. *Personality and Social Psychology Bulletin, 34*(3), 407–418. https://doi.org/10.1177/014616720
7311534

Groger, L., Mayberry, P. S., & Straker, J. K. (1999). What we didn't learn because of who would not talk to us. *Qualitative Health Research, 9,* 829–835. https://doi.org/10.1177/104973299129122180

Grosmaire, K., & French, N. (2016). *Forgiving my daughter's killer: A true story of loss, faith, and unexpected grace.* Thomas Nelson.

Gross, S., & Matheson, D. J. (2003). What they say at the end: Capital victims' families and the press. *Cornell Law Review, 88,* 486–516. http://
dx.doi.org/10.2139/ssrn.415081

Hechler, S., Funk, F., & Kessler, T. (2023). Not revenge, but change is sweet: Experimental evidence of how offender change and punishment play independent roles in victims' sense of justice. *British Journal of Social Psychology, 62,* 1013–1035. https://doi.org/10.1111/bjso.12613

Hochstetler, A. (2001). Reporting of executions in US newspapers. *Journal of Crime and Justice, 24*(1), 1–13. https://doi.org/10.1080/07356
48X.2001.9721614

Hodgkinson, P., Kandelia, S., & Reddy, R. (2009). Capital punishment: Creating more victims? In N. Loucks, S. Smith Holt, & J. R. Adler (Eds.), *Why we kill: Understanding violence across cultures and disciplines* (pp. 65–82). Middlesex University Press.

Jaeger, M. (1998). The power and reality of forgiveness: Forgiving the murderer of one's child. In R. D. Enright & J. North (Eds.), *Exploring Forgiveness* (pp. 9–14). University of Wisconsin Press.

Johnson, B. (2009, June 12). Ala. killer who taunted victim's mom executed. *Associated Press Newswires*. Document APRS000020090612e56c0003w

Johnson, S. K., Zitzmann, B., & Flemate, N. (2023). Forgiveness as a component of spiritual change after the murder of a loved one. *Death Studies, 47*(1), 94–104. https://doi.org/10.1080/07481187.2021.2021568

Kanwar, V. (2001). Capital punishment as "closure": The limits of a victim-centered jurisprudence. *Review of Law & Social Change, 27*, 215–255.

Karremans, J. C., Van Lange, P. A. M., Ouwerkerk, J. W., & Kluwer, E. S. (2003). When forgiving enhances psychological well-being: The role of interpersonal commitment. *Journal of Personality and Social Psychology, 84*(5), 1011–1026. https://doi.org/10.1037/0022-3514.84.5.1011

Kenney, J. S. (2002). Metaphors of loss: Murder, bereavement, gender, and presentation of the 'victimized' self. *International Review of Victimology 9*(3), 219–251. https://doi.org/10.1177/026975800200900301

King, R. (2003). *Don't kill in our names: Families of murder victims speak out against the death penalty.* Rutgers University Press.

King, K. (2004). It hurts so bad: Comparing grieving patterns of the families of murder victims with those of families of death row inmates. *Criminal Justice Policy Review, 15*(2), 193–211. https//doi.org/10.1177/0887403404263625

Kitching, C. (2018, February 23). Killer screams "murderers" as he's executed by lethal injection after eating steak and ice cream as last meal. *Mirror*. www.mirror.co.uk/news/us-news/killer-screams-murderers-hes-executed-12074387#:~:text=Money-,Killer%20screams%20%22murderers%22%20as%20he%27s%20executed%20by%20lethal%20injection%20after,ice%20cream%20as%20last%20meal&text=A%20death%20row%20prisoner%20repeatedly,student%20almost%2025%20years%20ago.

Koenig, M. (2022, June 8). Arizona death row inmate spent 30 MINUTES advising executioners on how to get needle into his vein before he was put to death: 66-year-old killed girl, 8, in 1984. *DailyMail.com*. www.dailymail.co.uk/news/article-10895547/Arizona-set-execute-Frank-Atwood-killed-girl-1984.html

Laughon, K., Steeves, R. H., Parker, B., Knopp, A., & Sawin, E. M. (2008). Forgiveness, and other themes, in women whose fathers killed their mothers. *Advances in Nursing Science, 31*(2), 153–163. https//doi.org/10.1097/01.ANS.0000319565.68760.4d

Marcus, J., & Massie, G. (2021, July 1). Texas executes man who killed his pregnant wife and 5-year-old daughter. *Independent, UK*. www.independent.co.uk/news/world/americas/texas-executes-john-hummel-murder-b1875956.html

Ministry of Justice. (2020). *Code of practice for victims of crime in England and Wales.* https://assets.publishing.service.gov.uk/government/uploads/system/uploads/attachment_data/file/974376/victims-code-2020.pdf

Montada, L. (1994). Injustice in harm and loss. *Social Justice Research, 7*(1), 5–28. https://doi.org/10.1007/BF02333820

Murray, F. (2023). Figan Murray. *The Forgiveness Project.* www.theforgivenessproject.com/stories-library/figen-murray/

Orth, U. (2002). Secondary victimization of crime victims by criminal proceedings. *Social Justice Research, 15,* 313–325. https://doi.org/10.1023/A:1021210323461

Orth, U. (2004). Does perpetrator punishment satisfy victims' feelings of revenge? *Aggressive Behavior, 30*(1), 62–70. https://doi.org/10.1002/ab.20003

Petrucci, C. J. (2002). Apology in the criminal justice setting: Evidence for including apology as an additional component in the legal system. *Behavioral Sciences & the Law, 20*(4), 337–362. https://doi.org/10.1002/bsl.495

Randa, R., & Reyns, B. W. (2020). The physical and emotional toll of identity theft victimization: A situational and demographic analysis of the National Crime Victimization Survey. *Deviant Behavior, 41*(10), 1290–1304. https://doi.org/10.1080/01639625.2019.1612980

Rando, T. A. (1993). *Treatment of complicated mourning.* Research Press.

Reed, M. D., & Caraballo, K. (2022). Voice of the victims: Accounts of secondary victimization with the court system among homicide co-victims. *Journal of Interpersonal Violence, 37*(13–14). https://doi.org/10.1177/0886260521989732

Rheingold, A. A., Baddeley, J. L., Williams, J. L., Brown, C., Wallace, M. M., Correa, F., & Rynearson, E. K. (2015). Restorative retelling for violent death: An investigation of treatment effectiveness, influencing factors, and durability. *Journal of Loss and Trauma, 20,* 541–555. https://doi.org/10.1080/15325024.2014.957602

Saco, L., & Dirks, D. (2018). Closure and justice: A qualitative study of perspectives from homicide survivorship experts. *Violence and Victims, 33*(5), 830–854. https//doi.org/10.1891/0886-6708.VV-D-17-00002

Seligman, M. E. P., & Csikszentmihalyi, M. (2000). Positive psychology: An introduction. *American Psychologist, 55*(1), 5–14.

Sharpe, T. L. (2015). Understanding the sociocultural context of coping for African American family members of homicide victims: A conceptual model. *Trauma, Violence, & Abuse, 16*(1), 48–59. https//doi.org/10.1177/1524838013515760

Sherman, L. W., Strang, H., Angel, C., Woods, D., Barnes, G. C., Bennett, S., & Inkpen, N. (2005). Effects of face-to-face restorative justice on victims of crime in four randomized, controlled trials. *Journal of Experimental Criminology, 1,* 367–395. https://doi.org/10.1007/s11292-005-8126-y

Sims, B. (2009, January 15). Alabama executes man for 1982 murder. *AL. com.* www.al.com/spotnews/2009/01/callahan.html

Sprang, M. V., McNeil, J. S., & Wright Jr, R. (1989). Psychological changes after the murder of a significant other. *Social Casework, 70*(3), 159–164. https://doi.org/10.1007/s11292-005-8126-y

Stebbings, P. (2014, August 6). US state of Missouri executes convicted killer. *Agence France Presse.* Document AFPR000020140806ea86003uz

Strang, H., & Sherman, L. W. (2003). Repairing the harm: Victims and restorative justice. *Utah Law Review*, 15–42.

Sullivan, D. (2013, April 10). Larry Mann executed for Palm Harbor girl's 1980 killing. *Tampa Bay Times.* www.tampabay.com/news/publi csafety/crime/larry-mann-executed-for-palm-harbor-girls-1980-killing/ 2114432/

Texas Department of Criminal Justice. (2023). *Victim services division.* Texas Department of Criminal Justice, www.tdcj.texas.gov/divisions/ vs/viewing_executions.html

Thompson, H. (2022, August 26). Death row hammer killer's last words and final meal before execution. *Daily Star.* www.dailystar.co.uk/news/ world-news/death-row-hammer-killers-last-27845179

Umbreit, M. S., Bradshaw, W., & Coates, R. B. (1999). Victims of severe violence meet the offender: Restorative justice through dialogue. *International Review of Victimology, 6*(4), 321–343. https://doi.org/ 10.1177/026975809900600405

Van Denderen, M., de Keijser, J., Stewart, R., & Boelen, P. A. (2018). Treating complicated grief and posttraumatic stress in homicidally bereaved individuals: A randomized controlled trial. *Clinical Psychology and Psychotherapy, 25*(4), 497–508. https//doi.org/10.1002/cpp.2183

Vollum, S., & Longmire, D. R. (2007). Covictims of capital murder: Statements of victims' family members and friends made at the time of execution. *Violence and Victims, 22*, 601–619. https//doi.org/ 10.1891/088667007782312131

Watanabe, S., & Laurent, S. M. (2020). Feeling bad and doing good: Forgivability through the lens of uninvolved third parties. *Social Psychology, 51*(1), 35–49. https://doi.org/10.1027/1864-9335/a000390

Williams, J. E. (1984). Secondary victimization: Confronting public attitudes about rape. *Victimology, 9*, 66–81.

Witvliet, C., Ludwig, T. E., & Vander Laan, K. L. (2001). Granting forgiveness or harboring grudges: Implications for emotion, physiology, and health. *Psychological Science, 12*, 117–123. https://doi.org/10.1111/ 1467-9280.00320

Worthington, E. L., Jr. (1998). *Dimensions of forgiveness: Psychological research and theological perspectives.* Templeton Foundation Press.

Ysseldyk, R., Matheson, K., & Anisman, H. (2007). Rumination: Bridging a gap between forgiving, vengefulness, and psychological health. *Personality and Individual Differences, 42*, 1573–1584. https://doi.org/10.1016/j.paid.2006.10.032

Yu, M., Li, X., Lu, J., Wang, S., Zhang, L., & Ge, Q. (2023). Empathy or counter-empathy? The victims' empathic response toward offenders depends on their relationships and transgression severity. *Psychology Research and Behavior Management, 16,* 1355–1363. https://doi.org/10.2147/PRBM.S407271

Zimring, F. E. (2004). *The contradictions of American capital punishment.* Oxford University Press.

5 Implications for the death penalty and justice systems in general

The evidence from Chapters 3 and 4 indicates that not much reconciliation between offenders and covictims takes place at executions. More often than not, there is no reconciliation between these parties, and neither appears to be satisfied with the outcome. Covictims often come away from the execution disappointed or angry, and offenders tend to be more successful at sincerely expressing their love to their family members than showing genuine and effective remorse to the families of their victims. This is not to suggest that everyone *should* be happy with the outcome: It was designed as a brutal punishment for brutal crimes. Although one goal of capital punishment is consequentialist – to deter future criminals and protect society – another goal is simply one of retribution – to make offenders pay for their crimes, with the harshness of the punishment matching the severity of the crimes (Tullett, 2022). Redemption and reconciliation are not built into this model of justice.

Implications for capital punishment

If one believes in the idea of *lex talionis* – an eye for an eye – then, at least in theory, capital punishment meets its retributivist goal. People who are convicted of murder are themselves killed. Of course, this assumes that it can be accurately judged, not just beyond a *reasonable* doubt but beyond *any doubt at all*, that someone has committed murder. The fact that there have been 192 death row exonerations since 1973 (Death Penalty Information Center, 2023) proves that this assumption is faulty. And while it is unlikely that

DOI: 10.4324/9781003384946-5

all of the 146 (13%) of inmates who claim they are innocent in their final statement actually are innocent, estimates show that as many as 4% of those on death row could be (Gross et al., 2014). Others have discussed in depth the practical and moral flaws of the retributivist goal of capital punishment (e.g., Nathanson, 2001), and since the data from the offender and covictim statements do not speak to it, we won't discuss it further here.

The data from both offenders and victims do, however, speak to the consequentialist goal of capital punishment. The consequentialist approach suggests that the death penalty is practical – it permanently removes dangerous individuals from society, thus guaranteeing that they will not be able to cause any further harm (Wood, 2010). The rationale here is that the only way to protect society from these dangerous individuals is to execute them. One obvious argument against this rationale is that a sentence of life without parole would have the same effect, although life without parole has been argued to be similarly problematic to the death penalty from a moral and ethical standpoint (Appleton & Grøver, 2007; Nellis, 2012). Two other arguments, however, can be made using the findings of the content analyses of the offenders' last statements summarized in Chapter 3 and the covictims' statements to the media in Chapter 4.

The fallacy of the unrepentant offender

The findings on the offenders' last statements before they are executed call into question the classification of individuals on death row as being uniformly dangerous and unredeemable. The seriousness of their crimes (assuming they were not falsely convicted) is undeniable: given that they committed a capital offence (i.e., murder with aggregating factors), they were clearly dangerous at the time of the offence. Not all dangerous individuals are sentenced to death, however. When juries (and sometimes judges) choose the death penalty over a long prison sentence for capital offenders, they have determined that the individual is not only dangerous but also unrepentant and incapable of redemption. Those who feel no remorse, it is argued, are more likely to reoffend and thus should be executed. The problem with this argument is that although they may not have expressed remorse during the trial (for the reasons outlined in Chapter 2), some offenders do appear to be remorseful at the time of their execution. Either they were remorseful at the time of their trial but were unable to convince the jury of this, or they developed remorse while they were in prison. Recall that 30% of inmates, when they had one final opportunity to make a statement before being executed, chose to apologize for their crimes. Sometimes these apologies were accompanied by other indicators of remorse and showed clear signs of genuine regret, shame, and sincerity. Considering how difficult it must be to generate an articulate, sincere, and convincing apology when one is about to be executed and under enormous stress, it is remarkable that any of them were able to show their remorse.

In addition to apologizing, 12% of the inmates took responsibility for their crimes. Being capable of recognizing the harm one has caused and taking ownership of it is recognized by forensic psychiatrists as a pathway towards pro-social identity change (Ferrito et al., 2017). Programmes designed to help violent offenders make meaning of their past have been successful at helping them develop a sense of personal agency and come to a better understanding of why they committed the crime, which then helps them to form healthy relationships and recognize their role in society as a moral citizen (Adshead, 2011; Adshead et al., 2018). Taking responsibility for our actions means that we recognize that we have control over them. Self-efficacy – our belief that we have control over our actions – has been shown to affect how we think, feel, and behave (Bandura, 1990). Research has shown that when criminal offenders believe they can successfully desist from engaging in crime they are less likely to reoffend (Johnston et al., 2019). This is not to suggest that all violent offenders have strong beliefs in their ability to refrain from committing crimes and thus might be redeemable, but it does show that some of them might. The consequentialist assumption that all offenders on death are dangerous does not seem to be supported by their last statements, which show evidence of regret, remorse, and personal agency.

Misjudging what covictims want and need

The consequentialist goal is to protect society. This assumes that a death sentence is better for society, without taking into consideration the needs or desires of some members of that society. Currently, 55% of Americans are in favour of capital punishment, but that leaves a large number of individuals who are not in favour of it and presumably do not feel better protected by it. Even covictims are not united in their desire to see the offender put to death. Some of them are opposed to the death penalty in principle, and others do not wish it for their specific situation (King, 2003). An alternative justice option, rather than the death penalty, might have made these individuals feel better protected.

Even though in their statements to the media covictims sometimes express relief after the execution and say that they felt safer knowing the offender was dead, their comments also indicate that they are not necessarily well-served by attending the execution. Sometimes they want, and receive, an apology from the offender (and for some it is one of the reasons they attend the execution) and sometimes they forgive, but this is not very common. More often, covictims seem to come away from the execution feeling disappointed, angry, and vengeful rather than with a sense of forgiveness or closure. Research that has shown that active participation in the justice system can make covictims feel worse rather than better (Buiter et al., 2022), and it has been suggested that what covictims need is better support services and communication rather than "legal measures intended to provide closure" (Saco & Dirks, 2018, p. 833). The death penalty does not seem to meet the consequentialist goal of protecting covictims; in fact, it might do the opposite.

Reconciling the motivations of offenders and the needs of covictims

Why don't more offenders apologize?

The analysis of their final statements showed that 30% of offenders apologized in their final statement. The case has been made that, given the many challenges they must face at the time of their execution, 30% is a reasonable number. However, this still leaves 70% who do not apologize. Even removing the 13% who say they are innocent and thus would not be expected to apologize, this still leaves more than half who do not even say the words "I'm sorry" to the family and other loved ones of the person they murdered.

It is possible that they did not apologize in their last statements because they had already apologized. Some inmates had been in contact with their victim's family before the execution, and some of them mentioned that they had written letters to the family. While we do not have data on how many fall into this category, it was clear in some instances, by the offender's last statement or the covictim's statement to the media, that this was the case. It is also possible that the inmate knew that the covictims were not present at the execution and would not hear their apology, so they did not bother making one. Some might have thought that the covictims would not accept their apology, so they chose not to make one rather than make one and have it be rejected. It might also be that they were overwhelmed by the situation and apologizing was not foremost in their mind. They might have been seeing their own family members for the first time in a long time and prioritized expressing their love and gratitude to them over addressing the covictims.

Notwithstanding the reasons outline in Chapter 2 as to why offenders might not apologize, many of the reasons listed earlier are directly related to the limitations of the situation. The execution chamber is not an ideal place for offenders to show their remorse. They might be frightened, uncertain, and/or angry. They are strapped to a gurney, and this might make them physically uncomfortable and prevent them from being able to see the witnesses. They also know that it is not a private event: even though the execution itself is not public, what they say will be made public by the members of the press who are in attendance. For all of these reasons, it might not seem to make sense to look for remorse in the last words of inmates before they are executed, but unfortunately it is one of the very few places where they have the opportunity to express it.

Why don't more covictims forgive?

There is no right or wrong way for covictims to feel about the person who killed their loved one. Even though this section considers the reasons why covictims might not forgive, it is not meant to imply that they should forgive. First and foremost, forgiveness is a choice, and choosing not to forgive might be just as beneficial for one individual as choosing to forgive might be for another. Each of these crimes was comprised of a different set of circumstances, including the events leading up to it and the aftermath, the response of the legal system, and the relationships of the people involved. As such, the covictims' statements to the media after witnessing the execution were diverse, and even though there are certain themes that connect many of the statements, every response to this unimaginable situation was unique. A broad recommendation for all of them to forgive would be both misguided and disrespectful. Asking why they do not forgive is simply intended as a way to understand their varied responses to the offender and the execution.

As diverse as their situations were, one thing that clearly united covictims was their grief. Despite their feelings about the offender and the justice system, what was most apparent in their statements was their love for the person they had lost and the huge impact it had on their lives. Even though for some of them the crime had taken place more than a decade earlier, their statements reflected a still-raw sense of loss and sorrow. Witnessing the execution would have been difficult, even if they felt it was truly justified, and it is important to remember that these complex emotions were underlying their response to the media following the execution.

Covictims expressed a lot of anger and negative emotions in their statements to the press after witnessing the execution. While it might be tempting to conclude from this that there is no hope of forgiveness for death row offenders from their victims' families, this is not necessarily the case. Although the number of offenders who asked for forgiveness and the number of covictims who forgave was relatively small, there was a connection between the two: Covictims were more likely to report having forgiven the offender if the offender specifically asked for forgiveness.

One reason why covictims might not forgive is that forgiveness is a process that occurs over time (McCullough et al., 2003). Although covictims would have been dealing with their loss for a long time (13.5 years, on average), the execution may be the first time they actually hear an apology from the offender. Apologies are not necessary for forgiveness to occur but they do help. If a covictim received an apology from the offender at the execution, without having had the opportunity to hear from the offender previously, it seems unlikely that the covictim would immediately forgive. What might be more likely is that the covictim could, over time, perhaps become more forgiving, or at least less angry and vengeful, towards the offender. Therefore, the positive effects of death row apologies on covictims may not be immediately apparent, but it does not necessarily mean that apologies have no impact.

The case for restorative justice in capital cases

Restorative justice provides an opportunity for those impacted by a crime to come together for meaningful dialogue in a controlled setting with the help of a trained facilitator (Zehr, 2015). One original purpose of restorative justice is to come to an agreement about restitution – the victim, the offender, and the community decide together how best for the offender to take responsibility for the crime and be reintegrated back into the community. In capital cases and other situations where the punishment has already been determined through the traditional justice system, restitution is not a focus but there are other principles and practices of restorative justice that can be applied. Victim-offender mediation and dialogue (VOMD) has been used to provide the opportunity for a meaningful, in-person discussion between the offender and those impacted by the crime, which can encourage offenders to take responsibility for their actions and help humanize them to victims (Umbreit & Vos, 2000). When it takes place after sentencing it can be more effective than a courtroom apology for many reasons, but one main consideration is that because it can no longer affect their sentence, the apology might be perceived as being more genuine (Szmania & Mangis, 2005).

While the full restorative justice model has not been used extensively in capital cases, there is some evidence that a modified version of it where covictims can meet offenders face-to-face before the execution can be beneficial (Umbreit & Vos, 2000; Walters, 2015). One important potential benefit of restorative justice is that it gives the offender the opportunity to apologize in person. If covictims want, or at least may come to appreciate, an apology from the offender, this opportunity could be invaluable. It would give covictims time to process the apology before the execution, which might change the dynamic during the execution. It would reduce the uncertainty of wondering whether and how the offender will apologize in his or her last statement and may even lead to a better understanding of the offender in those final moments. Meeting in person would allow the offender to more genuinely convey remorse, with the added benefit of having a better opportunity to display non-verbal indicators or remorse. If covictims choose to attend the execution specifically because they want to hear the offender apologize, perhaps if they already received an apology during the restorative justice process they would feel less inclined to attend. Given that attending the execution did not have many positive outcomes for covictims (and, in fact, may have distinctly negative outcomes), giving them less incentive to attend the execution could actually be beneficial for them.

Forgiveness is not a specified goal of restorative justice, and it is possible that an offender might participate in it but not apologize, and it is also possible that offender might apologize but the covictims might not accept the apology. Even if no forgiveness takes place, there are still potential benefits to all of the parties who participate in restorative justice. Simply being able to talk and ask questions can help with the healing process, and it might enable meaningful connections, if not with the offender, then perhaps with the offender's family, or other family members or friends of the victim (Walters, 2015). Another benefit of restorative justice is that it brings together all of the individuals affected by the crime. The offender's family are often overlooked during discussions of capital punishment, but they are also affected by it (Rossi, 2008). Not only are they dealing with the shame and guilt of having a loved one commit such an egregious act, but they are also aware that they are about to lose this person forever (Eschholz et al., 2003). The opportunity to meet the covictims and share their sorrow has the potential to help both parties: Covictims can learn more about the history of the offender, which might help humanize the offender to them, the offender's family can express their remorse for the offender's actions, and both parties might find common ground in their shared grief (Beck et al., 2007).

Although full restorative justice initiatives are rare in capital cases, there are variations of it already in place in many states with the death penalty. For example, defense-initiated victim outreach (DIVO) programmes exist at both the federal and state level (Bureau of Justice Assistance, 2023). These programmes are designed to address the needs of victims by providing a link between the offender (through the defence team) and the survivors of the victim. This usually begins early in the justice process, where a victim outreach specialist will reach out to victims to offer them the opportunity to share information, ask questions, and generally have a voice in the process. There are many potential benefits for victims: It can help them feel heard, validated, and understood, and it serves as a means to provide information to the victim regarding the progress of the legal proceedings, the defense strategy, and any available resources or support services. This transparency can help alleviate some of the uncertainties and anxieties victims may face during the criminal justice process. Although DIVO programmes are voluntary, Cantacuzino (2014) reports that in Texas, 54% of covictims in capital cases agreed to participate in it.

The case against restorative justice in capital cases

Not all covictims are interested in having contact with the person who murdered their loved one, and they might have very strong feelings about not wanting to see or hear from them. Offenders also might not be interested in participating in a restorative justice conference. First and foremost, restorative justice must be voluntary for both covictims and offenders. Therefore, it is not a realistic option for all capital cases. There is also the chance that being in contact with the offender might make victims feel worse. Although trained facilitators prepare participants for what to expect (and what not to expect) from the process and there is always a mediator present, covictims might be upset by what the offender says or does not say. Although covictims would be counselled not to expect an apology, they may want one anyway and would be disappointed if the offender does not seem remorseful. They may be hoping for a clear explanation of why the offender committed the crime, but the offender might not have an obvious reason or might be unable to articulate it.

An argument can also be made that restorative justice is impossible when the offender is on death row. By its definition, restorative justice is about *restoration* – finding a way for the offender to try to repair the harm they have caused and eventually be reintegrated into the community. Neither is possible if the offender is about to be executed. Although they may be able to provide some relief to covictims by giving them information and listening to them explain how the crime impacted them, and possibly even taking responsibility for the crime and offering a genuine apology, they cannot realistically atone for their crime. Radelet and Borg (2000) suggest that pairing restorative justice with the death penalty is at odds with the underlying goal of restorative justice to serve as an alternative to the traditional retributive model. By executing the offender regardless of what happens at the meetings between the covictims and the offender, the ultimate power remains with the government. Radelet and Borg (2000) argue that

> by its very nature, the death penalty is not about forgiveness (however conceptualized), finding common ground, or reconciliation. Instead, it embraces the polar opposites: retribution, hatred, and denial of the offender's humanity.
>
> (p. 90)

Identifying the inconsistency between the death penalty and restorative justice is more of a criticism of capital punishment than a statement on the ineffectiveness of restorative justice. This disconnect does not prevent covictims and offenders from benefitting from restorative justice initiatives, even if the ultimate fate of the offender is in direct opposition to the spirit of restorative justice. In interviews with 52 covictims whose offenders had been executed, some were empathetic towards the offender and open to forgiveness – even though they still supported the death penalty – especially those who had been given the opportunity to meet with the offender prior to the execution (Barrile, 2015). An in-depth case study of two victim-offender mediation sessions with covictims and death row inmates who were about to be executed found that both covictims and offenders reported a high level of satisfaction with the process and felt that it had helped in the healing process (Umbreit & Vos, 2000). Pointing to these encouraging findings, Umbreit (2000) states that any type of restorative programming is better than nothing:

> Who among us would be willing to deny an opportunity for a death row inmate and the victims/survivors of this criminal behavior to encounter each other's humanity, compassion, and strength as they help each other experience a greater sense of wholeness and healing, even if one party will lose his life through intentional state murder?
>
> (p. 95)

Even if they do not strictly fit with the underlying philosophy of restorative justice, the potential benefits, for those who want to participate, are undeniable. Making space in the capital punishment process for restorative justice initiatives, even more cost-effective modified restorative justice programmes like DIVO, is a compassionate response to a process that might feel very lacking in compassion.

Beyond capital punishment: Implications for the justice system in general

The United States is the only Western democratic nation that still engages in capital punishment. While there are other non-Western nations with death penalty laws – in 2022 China, Iran, Saudi Arabia, and Egypt executed more individuals than the United States (Amnesty International, 2023) – death row last statements from these executions and covictim interviews with the media are difficult or impossible to obtain. In addition, their legal systems, the crimes that are eligible for the death penalty, their processes for sentencing someone to death, and even their methods of execution may be very different from those described in this book. Therefore, the data described in Chapters 3 and 4, and the conclusions that can be derived from them, are specific to the United States. They cannot speak to the experiences of the individuals who are executed in other countries or the loved ones of their victims.

Although the findings may not generalize to other death penalties in other countries, they can help us understand the needs of victims and offenders in general, beyond the context of capital punishment. To be sure, there are certain aspects of the death penalty that are completely unique within systems of justice. For example, unlike other punishments, it is irreversible. It is impossible to undo an execution if it is later discovered that the inmate has been wrongfully convicted. There is also no hope for rehabilitation and eventual release – there are no programmes or resources to help them reintegrate back into society when they are released because they will never be released. Capital punishment also raises ethical and moral concerns far beyond those associated with the general idea of retributive (punishment-based) justice. That being said, the death penalty is still rooted in the justice system, and thus follows a similar process in terms of basic legal principles such as the burden of proof and the presumption of innocence until proven guilty. This justifies the consideration of how the findings in this book might inform justice systems in general.

The research and data presented in this book support two very clear conclusions: Some offenders – even those who commit horrific crimes – want to apologize, and some victims might benefit from hearing these apologies. If perpetrators of some of the worst types of crime imaginable can show signs of genuine remorse, it seems safe to assume that perpetrators of less heinous crimes might too. Knowing that even the survivors of murder victims might benefit more from having the opportunity to have an authentic conversation with the offender than from a harsher form of punishment suggests that efforts to be tougher on crime or impose mandatory minimum sentences under the guise of helping victims might be misguided. Below are four suggestions for how these findings could be incorporated into any system of justice, regardless of the degree of seriousness of the crime or the country in which the crime was committed.

Provide more opportunities for offenders to apologize

Between the years of 1976 and 2022, 30% of inmates on death row used their final words to apologize to their victims' families, and there were strong indicators that their apologies were sincere. Tragically, this may have been the first time that some of these offenders had been given the chance to address the covictims. Those who do not end up on death row face similar obstacles if they wish to apologize. The current system offers few opportunities for offenders to express their remorse directly to the victim(s), and those opportunities that do exist (e.g., in the courtroom, before sentencing) are less than ideal. Ironically, they may have even fewer opportunities to apologize than offenders on death row because they are never in the position to make a final statement. While some victims may consider an apology from an offender mean- ingless no matter how early in the process it is offered, there are victims who could directly benefit from learning that the offender feels remorseful, and there are some offenders who could directly benefit from being able to express their feelings to their victims.

This, of course, is not a new suggestion. Restorative justice researchers and practitioners have advocated for processes that do not isolate victims from offenders, and have developed many innovative programmes that allow for both parties to interact so that they can better understand the impacts of the crime on each other. There is convincing research that attests to the potential benefits of these programmes (for a review, see Latimer et al., 2005).

Do not assume that victims benefit from harsher punishment for offenders

One relatively surprising result of the analysis of covictims' comments to the media is that they do not appear to benefit from witnessing executions. They do report that they feel a sense of justice, but they also express revenge, disappointment, and anger towards both the offender and the process. These findings may help inform the discussion of whether victims benefit from harsher sentences for offenders. Statistics show that harsher punishments do not act as a deterrent for offenders (Bun et al., 2020; Doob & Webster, 2003), but less attention has been paid to the effect on the victims of crime. What little research has been done suggests that, although victims do often want revenge against offenders (Vidmar, 2001), their desire for revenge is not completely satisfied by the sentence imposed by the court, even if it is severe (Orth, 2004). This may be because the court system of imposing punishment based on the objective severity of the crime does not necessarily match what victims want. Research on the psychology of justice suggests that when victims (and even uninvolved third parties) desire justice after an offence it is in response to an intuitive, automatically produced sense of moral outrage rather than a reasoned response (Darley, 2009). In other words, the desire for justice is an unconscious process that does not involve a careful weighing of the offender's culpability or the severity of the crime. Punishment is not a "zero sum game" in which incremental increases in penalties for the offender result in equivalent benefits for victims (Zimring, 2001, p. 164).

If the justice system aims to take victim satisfaction and well-being into account, then it needs to understand what victims actually want and need. This also assumes that all victims want the same thing. Although many of the covictims who spoke to the media expressed support for the execution, some of them did not. The existence of groups such as Murder Victims' Families for Human Rights (mvfr.org) demonstrates that covictims are not united in their desire for death as punishment. If, as shown in our analysis of statements made by the loved ones of murder victims, even pro-death penalty covictims were not entirely well-served by the ultimate punishment of a death sentence, what evidence is there that harsher punishments and mandatory minimum sentences will satisfy victims of non-capital offences?

Reconsider involving victims in the punishment phase of the justice process

One reason for permitting covictims to be present for the execution is to provide them with closure, and also, more generally, to make them feel that they are involved in the punishment of the offender (Kanwar, 2001). However, a clear finding from the death row narratives is that the closure argument is not valid: covictims do not, as a rule, get closure from witnessing the offender's execution. In fact, it may be a mistake to consider closure as a valid and realistic outcome at all for victims of crime: Many covictims rejected the notion of closure outright, saying that they would never get closure or that it would only come when they died. The rhetoric on closure as being a primary "need" for victims comes in part from public opinion, and this public opinion, in turn, can influence public policy.

While involving victims in the process may be good for victims, the ways that they are permitted to be involved should be carefully considered. Currently one of the most common ways that victims are involved in the justice process is to provide a victim impact statement. These statements, most often provided before the sentencing phase of the trial, provide victims with an opportunity to express the emotional, physical, and financial impact of the crime on their lives. The stated purpose of victim impact statements is to give victims a voice in the criminal justice process and help inform judges and other relevant parties when determining an appropriate sentence (Cassell, 2008). It has been argued, however, that they do not effectively do either. Not only may victim impact statements not properly inform judges and juries, in part because of racial and other biases that affect which victims are encouraged to provide a statement (Bandes, 2022; Mundy, 2020), but they are also not uniformly therapeutic for the victims who give them. The victims who choose to provide a victim impact statement tend to be higher in anger and anxiety than those who do not, and they remain so after giving their statement (Buiter et al., 2022; Lens et al., 2015).

After a traumatic event, individuals often have a need to share their feelings about their experience (Curci & Rimé, 2012), and victims of crime are no different. Victim impact statements may not be the best way to do this because they might actually serve to fuel victims' anger rather than reduce it, in part because victims might feel the need to use the statement to ensure that the offender receives a harsher punishment. Studies have shown that the aspects of victim impact statements that victims do benefit from are that they allow them to have their voices heard and that they might prompt the offender to apologize (Rossi, 2008). This could be done more effectively after sentencing, with some type of victim-offender dialogue. For those who are angry, this would still allow them to share their feelings with the offender and, possibly, a wider audience, and for those who are not angry, it might allow them to have some form of reconciliation with the offender, and perhaps even get an apology.

Provide more support for restorative justice programmes

The above three recommendations can be summed up in this final point: although restorative justice may not be the best approach in all situations, it is not currently being used to its full potential. The death row data shows that some offenders were truly remorseful, and that some covictims forgave them. Had they been offered the opportunity to express these sentiments to each other in a safe environment before the execution, both parties may have benefited. Offenders may have been able to make peace with themselves and those they hurt, which may have helped them as they faced their execution. Covictims may have been able to attend the execution with less anger and desire for revenge (or, better yet, they may have felt less of a need to witness the execution), which may have helped them find some sort of closure or peace. In fact, some jurisdictions in the United States currently offer some restorative justice programmes on death row, and it will be important to examine the outcomes of these programmes once they have been in place long enough to generate empirical data.

These extreme cases show that some individuals who have lost a loved one to murder are able to find some kind of peace with the offender. Clearly, then, there is reason to believe that some victims of less severe crimes may also be able to find peace with the offender, and perhaps even forgive. Making restorative justice programmes more available, in cases where they are appropriate (i.e., the offender is remorseful and the victim is willing to listen to the offender), may seem like an obvious recommendation, but it bears repeating in as many different contexts as possible.

Conclusion

Studies of conflict demonstrate that remorse can be a powerful tool for reconciliation. When the person who has committed the offence clearly demonstrates that they feel remorse, they are acknowledging that they violated a moral code and that they pledge to work towards being better in the future. This allows the harmed person to let go of their anger and see the offender as a person who made a mistake but who still shares their goals, and hopefully will forgive them. In a sense, this process is about connecting through a shared sense of humanity. Social scientists have presented convincing evidence of this process for interpersonal, non-criminal transgressions, while noting that it can be affected by certain conditions, such as when the transgression is severe or intentional. Transgressions that are criminal in nature add a level of complexity to this model because they are often both severe and intentional, but there is also evidence that remorse can play an important role even when the transgression is a criminal offence.

Capital punishment presents an even greater challenge to this model of remorse and reconciliation, in part because it involves the most severe crimes and in part because the punishment of death is seen as being at odds with any form of remorse or reconciliation. In order for an individual to receive a death penalty, the legal system has determined that they are unredeemable. This label implies many things: a lack of remorse, the inability to understand the consequences of their actions, a disregard for human life, and a lack of humanity, to name a few. This is clearly not the type of individual who is capable of admitting that they violated a moral code and pledges to do better in the future. The survivors of their crimes – those whose loved ones were the victims of homicide – are rarely seen as being able to let go of their anger and seeing the offender as a person who made a mistake but who still shares their goals. Instead they are seen as passive victims who require the state to execute the offender so they can obtain closure.

The evidence presented in this book challenges these stereotypes. In their last statements, some offenders apologized, took responsibility for their crimes, and very clearly seemed to understand (and regret) the effects their actions had on the families and other loved ones of their victims. This remorse was apparent despite the context in which it had to be offered – in an execution chamber, surrounded by witnesses to their imminent death. The covictims, in their interviews with the media after witnessing the execution, did not overwhelmingly state that they felt closure, and in some cases they denied the possibility of closure at all.

Just because some of the individuals on death row and their covictims defy these stereotypes does not necessarily mean that remorse and reconciliation should occur when such a heinous crime has been committed, but it does suggest that they are possible, in some situations. Reconciliation, of course, does not mean that offenders will be released from prison and develop a close relationship with covictims. In the context of capital punishment, the meaning of reconciliation is more symbolic, implying that all parties come to acknowledge their shared humanity and perhaps replace feelings of anger and shame with less intense or neutral feelings. Individual cases studies (e.g., those described in TheForgivenessProject.com, or those interviewed by King, 2003 and Umbreit & Vos, 2000) have already shown that some covictims and offenders can benefit from this process. The evidence suggested here simply adds to the existing work that aims to better understand the connections between offenders and victims by taking a more trauma-informed, relational approach.

References

Adshead, G., (2011). The life sentence: Using a narrative approach in group psychotherapy with offenders. *Group Analysis, 44*(2), 131–244. https://doi-org.libproxy.wlu.ca/10.1177/0533316411400969

Adshead, G., Berko, Z., Bose, S., Ferrito, M., & Mindang, M. (2018). Is there a murderer here? The language of agency and violence in homicide perpetrators. In J. Adlam, T. Kluttig, & B. X. Lee (Eds.), *Violent states and creative states: From the global to the individual* (pp. 53–640). Kingsley.

Amnesty International. (2023). Death penalty. *Amnesty International.* www.amnesty.org/en/what-we-do/death-penalty/

Appleton, C., & Grøver, B. (2007). The pros and cons of life without parole. *The British Journal of Criminology*, *47*(4), 597–615. doi:10.1093/bjc/azm001

Bandes, S. A. (2022). What are victim impact statements for? *Brooklyn Law Review*, *87*(4), 1253–1282.

Bandura, A. (1990). Perceived self-efficacy in the exercise of personal agency. *Journal of Applied Sport Psychology*, *2*(2), 128–163. https://doi.org/10.1080/10413209008406426

Barrile, L. G. (2015). I forgive you, but you must die: Murder victim family members, the death penalty, and restorative justice. *Victims & Offenders*, *10*(3), 239–269. https://doi.org/10.1080/15564886.2014.925022

Beck, E., Britto, S., & Andrews, A. (2007). *In the shadow of death: Restorative justice and death row families.* Oxford University Press.

Buiter, M. Y., Boelen, P. A., Kunst, M., Gerlsma, C., de Keijser, J., & Lenferink, L. I. M. (2022). The mediating role of state anger in the associations between intentions to participate in the criminal trial and psychopathology in traumatically bereaved people. *International Journal of Law and Psychiatry*, *85*, 1–7. https://doi.org/10.1016/j.ijlp.2022.101840

Bun, M. J., Kelaher, R., Sarafidis, V., & Weatherburn, D. (2020). Crime, deterrence and punishment revisited. *Empirical Economics*, *59*, 2303–2333. https://doi.org/10.1007/s00181-019-01758-6

Bureau of Justice Assistance. (2023). Defense-initiated victim outreach. https://bja.ojp.gov/sites/g/files/xyckuh186/files/media/document/divo.pdf

Cantacuzino, M. (2014). Transforming lives through the power of personal narrative: Innovative restorative justice programs in custodial and community settings. *The Forgiveness Project.* http://theforgivenessproject.com/wp-content/uploads/2014/04/Churchill-Fellowship-Report_M-Cantacuzino.pdf

Cassell, P. G. (2008). In defense of victim impact statements. *Ohio State Journal of Criminal Law*, *6*, 611–648.

Curci, A., & Rimé, B. (2012). The temporal evolution of social sharing of emotions and its consequences on emotional recovery: A longitudinal study. *Emotion*, *12*(6), 1404–1414. https://doi.org/10.1037/a0028651

Darley, J. M. (2009). Morality in the law: The psychological foundations of citizens' desires to punish transgressions. *Annual Review of Law and Social Science*, *5*, 1–23. https://doi.org/10.1146/annurev.lawsocsci.4.110707.172335

Death Penalty Information Center. (2023). *Issues: Innocence.* https://deathpenaltyinfo.org/policy-issues/innocence

Doob, A. N., & Webster, C. M. (2003). Sentence severity and crime: Accepting the null hypothesis. *Crime and Justice, 30*, 143–195. https://doi.org/10.1086/652230

Eschholz, S., Reed, M. D., Beck, E., & Leonard, P. B. (2003). Offenders' family members' responses to capital crimes: The need for restorative justice initiatives. *Homicide Studies, 7*(2), 154–181. https//doi.org/10.1177/1088767902250819

Ferrito, M., Needs, A., & Adshead, G. (2017). Unveiling the shadows of meaning: Meaning-making for perpetrators of homicide. *Aggression and Violent Behavior, 34*, 263–272. https://doi.org/10.1016/j.avb.2016.11.009

Gross, S. R., O'Brien, B., Hu, C., & Kennedy, E. H. (2014). Rate of false conviction of criminal defendants who are sentenced to death. *Proceedings of the National Academy of Sciences, 111*(20), 7230–7235. https://doi.org/10.1073/pnas.1306417111

Johnston, T. M., Brezina, T., & Crank, B. R. (2019). Agency, self-efficacy, and desistance from crime: An application of social cognitive theory. *Journal of Developmental and Life-Course Criminology, 5*, 60–85. https://doi.org/10.1007/s40865-018-0101-1

Kanwar, V. (2001). Capital punishment as "closure": The limits of a victim-centered jurisprudence. *Review of Law & Social Change, 27*, 215–255.

King, R. (2003). *Don't kill in our names: Families of murder victims speak out against the death penalty*. Rutgers University Press.

Latimer, J., Dowden, C., & Muise, D. (2005). The effectiveness of restorative justice practices: A meta-analysis. *The Prison Journal, 85*(2), 127–144. https//doi.org/10.1177/0032885505276969

Lens, K. M., Pemberton, A., Brans, K., Braeken, J., Bogaerts, S., & Lahlah, E. (2015). Delivering a victim impact statement: Emotionally effective or counter-productive? *European Journal of Criminology, 12*(1), 17–34. https://doi.org/10.1177/1477370814538778

McCullough, M. E., Fincham, F. D., & Tsang, J. A. (2003). Forgiveness, forbearance, and time: the temporal unfolding of transgression-related interpersonal motivations. *Journal of Personality and Social Psychology, 84*(3), 540–557. https://doi.org/10.1037/0022-3514.84.3.540

Mundy, H. M. (2020). Forgiven, forgotten? Rethinking victim impact statements for an era of decarceration. *UCLA Law Review Discourse, 68*, 301–337.

Nathanson, S. (2001). *An eye for an eye: The immorality of punishing by death*. Rowman & Littlefield.

Nellis, A. (2012). Tinkering with life: A look at the inappropriateness of life without parole as an alternative to the death penalty. *University of Miami Law Review, 67*, 439–457.

Orth, U. (2004). Does perpetrator punishment satisfy victims' feelings of revenge? *Aggressive Behavior, 30*, 62–70. https://doi.org/10.1002/ab.20003

Radelet, M. L., & Borg, M. J. (2000). Comment on Umbreit and Vos: Retributive versus restorative justice. *Homicide Studies, 4*(1), 88–92. https://doi.org/10.1177/1088767900004001005

Rossi, R. A. (2008). Meet me on death row: Post-sentence victim-offender mediation in capital cases. *Pepperdine Dispute Resolution Law Journal, 9*(1), 185–210. https://digitalcommons.pepperdine.edu/drlj/vol9/iss1/6

Saco, L., & Dirks, D. (2018). Closure and justice: A qualitative study of perspectives from homicide survivorship experts. *Violence and Victims, 33*(5), 830–854. https//doi.org/10.1891/0886-6708.VV-D-17-00002

Szmania, S. J., & Mangis, D. E. (2005). Finding the right time and place: A case study comparison of the expression of offender remorse in traditional justice and restorative justice contexts. *Marquette Law Review, 89*(2), 335–358.

Tullett, A. M. (2022). The limitations of social science as the arbiter of blame: An argument for abandoning retribution. *Perspectives on Psychological Science, 17*(4), 995–1007. https://doi.org/10.1177/174569 16211033284

Umbreit, M. S. (2000). Reply to Radelet and Borg. *Homicide Studies, 4*(1), 93–97. https://doi.org/10.1177/1088767900004001006

Umbreit, M. S., & Vos, B. (2000). Homicide survivors meet the offender prior to execution: Restorative justice through dialogue. *Homicide Studies, 4*(1), 63–87. https://doi.org/10.1177/1088767900004001004

Vidmar, N. (2001). Retribution and revenge. In J. H. Sanders & V. Lee (Eds.), *Handbook of justice research in law* (pp. 31–63). Kluwer Academic Publishers.

Walters, M. A. (2015). 'I thought "he's a monster"…[but] he was just… normal': Examining the therapeutic benefits of restorative justice for homicide. *British Journal of Criminology, 55*(6), 1207–1225. doi:10.1093/bjc/azv026

Wood, D. (2010). Punishment: Consequentialism. *Philosophy Compass, 5*(6), 455–469. https://doi.org/10.1111/j.1747-9991.2010.00287.x

Zehr, H. (2015). *The little book of restorative justice: Revised and updated.* Simon and Schuster.

Zimring, F. E. (2001). Imprisonment rates and the new politics of criminal punishment. *Punishment & Society, 3*(1), 161–166.

Index

For Product Safety Concerns and Information please contact our EU
representative GPSR@taylorandfrancis.com
Taylor & Francis Verlag GmbH, Kaufingerstraße 24, 80331 München, Germany

www.ingramcontent.com/pod-product-compliance
Lightning Source LLC
Chambersburg PA
CBHW061749270326
41928CB00011B/2438